Law and Life

ROBERT M. HADDAD

Nihil Obstat: Rev. Peter Joseph, STD.

Imprimatur: + Julian Porteous, DD, VG,

Date: 13th November, 2003

The *Nihil Obstat* and *Imprimatur* are a declaration that a book or pamphlet is considered to be free from doctrinal or moral error. It is not necessarily implied that those who have granted them agree with the contents, opinions or statements expressed.

Scripture quotes taken from the ***Revised Standard Version of the Bible (Second Catholic Edition)***, copyright © 2006 (Ignatius Press).

Extracts from ***The Faith of the Early Fathers,*** Rev. William A. Jurgens, copyright © 1970 by The Order of St. Benedict, Inc., The Liturgical Press, Collegeville, Minnesota. Used with permission.

Extracts from ***The Roman Catechism***, Issued by order of Pope St. Pius V, 1566, reprinted by TAN Books and Publishers, Rockford, Illinois 61105.

Extracts from English translation of ***Catechism of the Catholic Church*** for Australia copyright © June 1994 St. Pauls/Libreria Editrice Vaticana. Used with permission.

Cover design: Parousia Media, PO Box 59, Galston, NSW, 2159.
www.parousiamedia.com

Published by: Parousia Media.

© Robert M. Haddad 2014. All rights reserved. Extracts and copies of various parts or chapters of the series may be made in cases of 'fair dealing', viz., for the purpose of teaching, promoting and defending the Catholic Faith. All acknowledgments given to Robert M. Haddad.

ISBN: 978-1-922660-60-2

Contents

Foreword	v
Part I – The Seven Sacraments	**1**
Introduction	2
Baptism	7
Confirmation	13
The Blessed Eucharist	19
Penance	26
Anointing of the Sick	31
Holy Orders	36
Holy Matrimony	43
Part II – The Ten Commandments	**51**
Introduction	52
The First Commandment	57
The Second Commandment	64
The Third Commandment	70
The Fourth Commandment	75
The Fifth Commandment	80
The Sixth Commandment	85
The Seventh Commandment	89
The Eighth Commandment	94
The Ninth and Tenth Commandments	98
Part III – The Lord's Prayer	**102**
Introduction	103
Our Father who Art in Heaven	108
Hallowed be Thy Name	112
Thy Kingdom Come	116
Thy Will be Done	121
Give us this Day our Daily Bread	126
And Forgive us our Trespasses	130
And Lead us Not into Temptation	134
But Deliver us from Evil. Amen.	138

Appendices 142

A. Council of Trent, Decree on Justification
   (On keeping the Commandments) 142
B. Magisterial Pronouncements on the Sacraments in General 145
C. Prayers 156

About the Author 160

Other Works by the Author 161

Foreword

If man knew his religion ...

"Neither wealth, nor honors, nor vanity can make a man happy during his life on earth, but only attachment to the service of God, when we are fortunate enough to realize that and to carry it out properly. The woman who is held in contempt by her husband is not unhappy in her state because she is held in contempt but because she does not know her religion or because she does not practise what her religion tells her she should do. Teach her her religion, and from the moment that you see her practise it, she will cease to complain and to consider herself unhappy. Oh! How happy man would be, even on this earth, if he knew his religion!

What power that person who is near to God possesses when he loves Him and serves Him faithfully! Alas, my dear brethren, anyone who is despised by worldly people, who appears to be unimportant and humble, look at him when he masters the very will and power of God Himself. Look at Moses, who compels the Lord to grant pardon to three hundred thousand men who were indeed guilty. Look at Josue, who commanded the sun to stand still and the sun became immobile, a thing which never happened before and which perhaps will never happen again. Look at the Apostles: simply because they loved God, the devils fled before them, the lame walked, the blind saw, the dead arose to life. Look at St Benedict, who commanded the rocks to stop in their course and they remained hanging in mid-air. Look at him who multiplied bread, who made water come out of the rocks, and who disposed of the stones and the forest as easily as if they were wisps of straw. Look at St Francis of Paula who commands the fish to come to hear the word of God and they respond to his call with such loyalty that they applaud his words. Look at St John who commands the birds to keep silent and they obey him. Look at many others who walk the seas without any human aid. Very well! Now take a look at all those impious people and all those famous ones of the world with all their wit and all their knowledge for achieving everything. Alas! Of what are they really capable? Of nothing at all. And why not? Unless it is because they are not attached to the service of God. But how powerful and how happy at the same time is the person who knows his religion and who practises what it commands ..."

Sermons of St John Vianney,
for the Fourteenth Sunday after Pentecost.

Part I

The Seven Sacraments

Introduction

"With joy you will draw water from the wells of salvation" (Is. 12:3).

The Sacraments are efficacious signs of grace instituted by Christ. They are external rites that both signify and confer the grace they signify. By grace is understood sanctifying grace and its concomitant supernatural virtues, seven gifts of the Holy Spirit, and actual graces needed to live as adopted children of God and heirs to heaven.

Grace is a supernatural reality that is beyond the grasp of our external senses. Hence, in His profound thoughtfulness Christ connected the bestowal of grace with material things such as water, oil, bread and wine to give consoling certainty through the senses of the precise moment when grace is bestowed. The Sacraments are thus appropriately fitted to our human nature comprised of body and soul.

God therefore as principal cause produces the most spiritually momentous effects through the most common of things as His instruments, giving them a power akin to His omnipotence. The Sacraments operate *ex opere operato*, that is by their very usage. Provided the recipient places no obstacle in the way, every sacrament properly administered bestows the grace intended.

It is the solemn teaching of the Catholic Church that there are seven sacraments, viz., Baptism, Confirmation, Blessed Eucharist, Penance, Anointing of the Sick, Holy Orders and Holy Matrimony.[1] They provide grace for every individual and community need from the cradle to the grave. Baptism gives the soul birth to the supernatural order and a participation in God's own life; the Eucharist gives daily supernatural nourishment and strength through union with Christ's Body, Blood, Soul and Divinity; Confirmation gives the seven gifts of the Holy Spirit in added strength to lead the life of an adult Christian courageously; Penance restores the Christian to the life of grace after it has been lost through mortal sin; Holy Matrimony gives the Christian couple the grace to raise and educate their children for God in a life-long indissoluble union modelled on Christ's union with the Church; Holy Orders enables

---

[1] Council of Trent, *Canons on the Sacraments in General*, Canon 1, 3 March, 1547.

the clergy to faithfully carry out their mission on earth as other Christs; and Anointing of the Sick assists the Christian to meet sickness and death with resignation, courage and peace of mind.

The Sacraments are constituted of *matter* and *form*. As mentioned above, the matter normally consists of a material thing or action such as water, oil, bread or wine, imposition of hands; while the form is comprised of a prescribed set of words. To alter substantially either the matter or the form of a sacrament in its administration would be to destroy its validity altogether. So to baptize one with oil rather than water would render the baptism null and void; likewise, if the minister were to employ words other than "in the name of the Father and of the Son and of the Holy Spirit" when pouring the water.

In Baptism, Confirmation, Anointing of the Sick and Holy Orders, the words are accompanied by a respective action: in Baptism, the pouring of water signifies spiritual cleansing; in Confirmation, the anointing with oil signifies spiritual strengthening; in Anointing of the Sick, healing; in Holy Order, the laying of hands signifies bestowal of the Holy Spirit. In the Eucharist, the bread and wine suggest spiritual food; in Penance, the sorrowful confession of guilt points to the absolution that follows; in Holy Matrimony, the exchange of vows signifies the union of Christ with His Church.

Three of the sacraments, namely Baptism, Confirmation and Holy Orders, confer a *character*. A character is an indelible mark imprinted on the soul that, so-to-speak, demands, and where there is no obstacle, gives grace to the soul, as well as a right to actual graces. It can never be removed, even by mortal sin. The characters given by Baptism, Confirmation and Holy Orders show that one belongs to Christ and respectively invest the Christian with a special office in the Church to receive, defend and administer divine things.

With the exception of Baptism and Holy Matrimony, the minister of the sacrament must be in Holy Orders. Baptism, in exceptional circumstances relating to emergency, may be administered by a member of the laity (or even a non-Catholic); Matrimony is conferred reciprocally by the man and woman entering the sacred contract.

The minister of the sacrament must:
(i) Employ the proper form of words.

(ii) Perform the prescribed action.
(iii) Use the prescribed matter.
(iv) Intend to do what the Church does.

It is not essential that the minister be in a state of grace or even personally believe in the rite. This is due to the fact that the virtue of the sacrament comes not from the minister, but from Christ.

To be eligible to receive any of the sacraments it is necessary that the candidate be first validly baptized "in the name of the Father and of the Son and of the Holy Spirit" (Mt 28:19). Normally, for worthy reception of a sacrament, the candidate must be in a state of grace, with the exception of Baptism and Penance where attrition alone is sufficient for worthy reception. The better the disposition of the candidate, the more grace is received. If there be no good dispositions then no grace is received. A person who knowingly and wilfully receives a sacrament in a state of mortal sin commits the grave sin of sacrilege.

Finally, as the Sacraments are the instruments by which Christ bestows His grace upon us, it follows that no one, however perfect their dispositions, can exhaust the grace that flows through them.

The Fathers

Tertullian, *The Resurrection of the Dead* 8, 3 (inter AD 208-212)
"The flesh, then, is washed, so that the soul may be made clean. The flesh is anointed so that the soul may be dedicated to holiness. The flesh is signed, so that the soul too may be fortified. The flesh is shaded by the imposition of hands, so that the soul too may be illuminated by the Spirit. The flesh feeds on the Body and Blood of Christ, so that the soul may be nourished on God."

St Cyprian of Carthage, *Letter to Januarius and the Bishops of Numidia* 70, 2 (AD 254-255)
"It is necessary for him that has been baptized also to be anointed, so that by his having received chrism, that is, the anointing, he can be the anointed of God and have in himself the grace of Christ. But in turn, it is by the Eucharist that the oil with which the baptized are anointed is

sanctified on the altar. He that has neither altar nor church, however, is not able to sanctify that creature, oil."

St Cyril of Jerusalem, *Catechetical Lectures* **1, 5 (c. AD 350)**
"Cleanse your vessel that you may receive grace more abundantly; for although the remission of sins is given to all equally, the communion of the Holy Spirit is bestowed in proportion to the faith of such. If you have labored little, you will receive little; but if your labor has been great, great will be your reward ... By the loving-kindness of God you have, in our former meetings, heard enough about Baptism and Chrism, and of the reception of the Body and Blood of Christ. And now it behoves us to pass on to what is next ..."

St Ambrose of Milan, *The Sacraments* **4, 4, 14 (AD 390-391)**
"Who, then, is the author of the Sacraments if not the Lord Jesus? Those Sacraments came from heaven; for every counsel is from heaven."

St Augustine of Hippo, *Baptism* **3, 10, 13 (AD 400)**
"It is one thing not to have something, and another to have it not by right or to usurp it illicitly. It is not that they are not the Sacraments of Christ and of the Church because they are used illicitly, and this not by heretics only, but by all the wicked and impious. Such persons ought to be corrected and punished, but the Sacraments should be acknowledged and revered."

St Augustine of Hippo, *Homilies on John* **15, 4 (AD 416-417)**
"What is the Baptism of Christ? 'The washing with water, in the word.' Take away water and it is not Baptism. Take away the word and it is not Baptism."

The Roman Catechism (1566)

Pt. II, Ch. I: The Sacraments of the Catholic Church are seven in number, as is proved from Scripture, from the tradition handed down to us from the Fathers, and from the authority of Councils. Why they are either more nor less in number may be shown, at least with some probability, from the analogy that exists between the natural and the spiritual life. In order to exist, to preserve existence, and to contribute to his own and to the public good, seven things seem necessary to man: to be born, to grow, to be nurtured, to be cured when sick, when weak to be strengthened; as far as regards the public welfare, to have magistrates invested with authority to govern, and to perpetuate himself and his species by legitimate offspring. Now, since it is quite clear that all these things are sufficiently analogous to that life by which the soul lives to God, we discover in them a reason to account for the number of the Sacraments.

Catechism of the Catholic Church (1992)

No. 1212: The sacraments of Christian initiation - Baptism, Confirmation, and the Eucharist - lay the *foundations* of every Christian life. The sharing of the divine nature given to men through the grace of Christ bears a certain likeness to the origin, development, and nourishing of natural life. The faithful are born anew by Baptism, strengthened by the sacrament of Confirmation, and receive in the Eucharist the food of eternal life. By means of these sacraments of Christian initiation, they thus receive in increasing measure the treasures of the divine life and advance toward the perfection of charity.

No. 1421: The Lord Jesus Christ, physician of our souls and bodies, who forgave the sins of the paralytic and restored him to bodily health, has willed that his Church continue, in the power of the Holy Spirit, his work of healing and salvation, even among her own members. This is the purpose of the two sacraments of healing: the sacrament of Penance and the sacrament of Anointing of the Sick.

No. 1534: Two other sacraments, Holy Orders and Matrimony, are directed towards the salvation of others; if they contribute as well to personal salvation, it is through service to others that they do so. They confer a particular mission in the Church and serve to build up the People of God.

Baptism

"Go therefore and make disciples of all nations, baptizing them in the name of the Father and of the Son and of the Holy Spirit" (Mt 28:19).

Baptism is the first of the sacraments by which we are made children of God, members of Christ's Mystical Body the Church, and hence Christians. Any person, child or adult, who has not been baptized can be a candidate to receive it.

Baptism is effected by the minister either immersing the candidate in natural water, or pouring water over the candidate, while reciting the following words: "N., I baptize you in the name of the Father and the Son, and of the Holy Spirit" (cf. Mt 28:19). It is easily apparent why Christ chose water as the matter of Baptism for it is so easy to procure, is necessary for life and has the effect of cleansing. God has elevated this most common of compounds by giving it the power to cleanse and give life to the human soul. The water must actually touch and flow over some part of the body.

In normal circumstances, Baptism is administered solemnly by one in Holy Orders with all the accompanying ceremonies prescribed by the Church. In cases of necessity, Baptism may be conferred privately by any person who has attained the age of reason. Necessity arises where there is immediate danger of death or where there is a shortage of ordained ministers such as in missionary countries.

During the baptismal ceremony, the candidate's body is anointed and signed with the Cross. The body is thus also consecrated to God and no longer a thing profane, but rather a sacred instrument belonging to Christ and a worthy companion of the soul.

In Acts 2:38; 10:48 we read of Baptism "in the name of Jesus Christ." This formula is employed by various Protestant denominations. This term was used by St Luke in Acts to distinguish Christ's baptism from St John the Baptist's, which did not bestow the Holy Spirit (Acts 19:1-2).

In becoming children of God we are supernaturally "born again" (or "born anew": Jn 3:3). In addition to being given the right to inherit God's Kingdom, the Holy Spirit Himself together with sanctifying grace come into our souls to remove all stain of sin, original and actual (mortal and venial), as well as extinguishing all debt of temporal punishment due in purgatory: "And Peter said to them, Repent, and be baptized every one of you in the name of Jesus Christ for the forgiveness of your sins; and you shall receive the gift of the Holy Spirit" (Acts 2:38); "Rise and be baptized, and wash away your sins, calling on his name" (Acts 22:16). With sanctifying grace, we also receive the supernatural virtues, the seven gifts of the Holy Spirit and sacramental grace, that is, the right to actual graces of union, light and fruitfulness to enable us to live the Christian life.

Baptism can be received only once as it effects a permanent change in the soul by imprinting a "character." This character can never be removed, not even by mortal sin. It is by virtue of the character that we become incorporated into Christ's Mystical Body and eligible to receive all the other sacraments. Furthermore, Baptism likens the Christian to Christ in His death and resurrection. As Christ died and rose but once, so too does the Christian die and rise only once in Baptism.

The Church teaches that for both adults and infants Baptism is necessary for salvation[1], for as the Scriptures say: "He who believes and is baptized will be saved ..." (Mk 16:16); "... unless one is born of water and the Spirit, he cannot enter the kingdom of God" (Jn 3:5); "Baptism, which corresponds to this, now saves you ..." (1 Pet. 3:21); and to the Apostles, "Go therefore and make disciples of all nations, baptizing them in the name of the Father and of the Son and of the Holy Spirit" (Mt 28:19). Christ, therefore, both established the rite and outlined how it was to be administered. Also, by adding "and lo, I am with you always, to the close of the age" (Mt 28:20), Christ showed that Baptism is to remain in the Church until He comes again in judgment at the end of the world.

Because of the necessity of Baptism, the Church requires that all infants be baptized "within the first weeks" (Canon 867). Where there is a danger of death the child should be baptized privately and without delay. Baptism of children is legitimate because they have original sin which is remitted by the rite, they have no impediment of actual sin to inhibit the infusion of sanctifying grace, they receive the imprint of the character, and the required faith is supplied by the Church through *sponsors* or God-

---

[1] Council of Trent, *Canons on the Sacrament of Baptism*, Canon 5, 3 March, 1547.

parents. Consequently, there is no reason to withhold the wonderful effects of Baptism from infants until they reach the age of reason. By baptizing infants, the Catholic Church frees them as soon as possible from the dominion of Satan and admits them into the company of children of God: "Let the children come to me, and do not hinder them; for to such belongs the kingdom of heaven" (Mt 19:14). Nowhere is it stated in Scripture that Baptism is administered only to adults.

It is part of the sponsor's office to make a profession of faith in the name of the baptized child during the ceremony and, together with the parents, help it to grow in and live a Christian life. A sponsor must be a confirmed Catholic of not less than sixteen years of age living a life of faith befitting the role to be undertaken. Parents of the person to be baptized cannot act as sponsors.

Children who have not been baptized and who have not committed any actual sin, according to St Augustine of Hippo, participate in the real, though only natural, happiness of *Limbo of the Unbaptized*. This is so because they are not born to the life of supernatural grace necessary to behold God face to face in the Beatific Vision. Another view asserts that, as God wills that "all men to be saved and to come to the knowledge of the truth" (1 Tim. 2:4), He will provide some means to glorify them so that they too may inherit heaven. If that be so, we have no sure way of knowing it, and cannot depend upon any theories. In any case, they are filled with happiness and enjoy God's presence. One thing is certain: they will all rise with immortal fully-grown bodies at the General Resurrection.

In the case of adult converts the *Catechumenate* occupies an important part in the preparation for Baptism. Catechumens should be properly formed in the whole Christian life in order to receive all three sacraments of initiation, namely, Baptism, Confirmation and Holy Communion and to bring their conversion to maturity.

The necessity of water baptism, however, does not exclude the efficacy of substitutes such as *Baptism of Desire* and *Baptism of Blood*. A person has a baptism of desire when he or she has perfect contrition for their sins and desires to do all necessary for salvation. Baptism of desire resembles sacramental Baptism in producing sanctifying grace in the soul and forgiving original sin and serious actual sin. This doctrine is proved from the following words of Christ: "he who loves me will be loved by my

Father, and I will love him and manifest myself to him" (Jn 14:21); "her sins, which are many, are forgiven, for she loved much" (Lk 7:47); "Truly, I say to you, today you will be with me in Paradise" (Lk 23:43).

A person has a baptism of blood when he or she is put to death for the Faith, that is, dies as a martyr. Christ has promised salvation to those who give their lives for Him: "he who loses his life for my sake will find it" (Mt 10:39); "every one who acknowledges me before men, I also will acknowledge before my Father who is in heaven" (Mt 10:32).

Unlike baptism of water neither baptism of desire nor baptism of blood imprint the sacramental character or officially and publicly make one a member of the Church, but Baptism of Blood does remit all temporal punishment due to sin.

The Fathers

The Didache 7, 1 (inter AD 90-150)
"Baptize thus: After the foregoing instructions, baptize in the name of the Father and of the Son, and of the Holy Spirit, in living water. If you have no living water, then baptize in other water; and if you are not able in cold, then in warm. If you have neither, pour water three times on the head, in the name of the Father, and of the Son, and of the Holy Spirit."

The Shepherd of Hermas Parables 9, 16, 2 (inter AD 140-155)
"They had need to come up through the water, so that they might be made alive; for they could not otherwise enter into the Kingdom of God except by putting away the mortality of their former life. These also, then, who had fallen asleep received the seal of the Son of God, and entered into the Kingdom of God. For before a man bears the name of the Son of God, he is dead. But when he receives the seal, he puts mortality aside and again receives life. The seal, therefore, is the water. They go down into the water dead, and come out of it alive."

St Justin Martyr, *First Apology* 61 (c. AD 155)
"Then they are led by us to a place where there is water; and there they are reborn in the same kind of rebirth in which we ourselves were reborn: in the name of God, the Lord and Father of all and of our Savior, Jesus

Christ, and of the Holy Spirit, they receive the washing with water. For Christ said, 'unless you be reborn, you shall not enter into the Kingdom of Heaven ...' The reason for doing this, we have learned from the Apostles."

St Cyprian of Carthage, *Letter to Jubaianus* 73, 22 (c. AD 254-256)
"(Catechumens who suffer martyrdom before they have received Baptism with water) are not deprived of the Sacrament of baptism. Rather, they are baptized with the most glorious and greatest Baptism of blood, concerning which the Lord said that He had another Baptism with which He Himself was to be baptized."

St Hippolytus of Rome, *The Apostolic Tradition* 21 (c. AD 215)
"Baptize first the children; and if they can speak for themselves, let them do so. Otherwise, let their parents or other relatives speak for them."

Origen, *Commentaries on Romans* 5, 8 (post AD 244)
"Why, when the Lord Himself told His disciples that they should baptize all peoples in the name of the Father and of the Son and of the Holy Spirit, does this Apostle employ the name of Christ alone in Baptism, saying, 'we who have been baptized in Christ;' for indeed, legitimate Baptism is had only in the name of the Trinity."

St Basil the Great, *The Holy Spirit* 12, 28 (AD 375)
"Let no one be misled by the fact that the Apostle frequently omits the name of the Father and of the Holy Spirit when mentioning baptism; nor let anyone suppose that the invocation of the Names is a matter of indifference ... The naming of Christ, you see, is the confession of the whole; it bespeaks the God who anoints, the Son who is anointed, and the Spirit who is the anointing ... If, then, in baptism the separation of the Spirit from the Father and the Son is perilous to the one baptizing and useless to the one receiving, how can it be safe for us to separate the Spirit from the Father and the Son?"

The Roman Catechism (1566)

Pt. II, Ch. II: If the knowledge of what has been hitherto explained be, as it is, of highest importance to the faithful, it is no less important to them to learn that the law of Baptism, as established by our Lord, extends to all, so that unless they are regenerated to God through the grace of Baptism, be their parents Christians or infidels, they are born to eternal misery and destruction. Pastors, therefore, should often explain these words of the Gospel: *Unless a man be born again of water and the Holy Ghost, he cannot enter into the Kingdom of God.*

Catechism of the Catholic Church (1992)

No. 1213: Holy Baptism is the basis of the whole Christian life, the gateway to life in the Spirit (*vitae spiritualis ianua*), and the door which gives access to the other sacraments. Through Baptism we are freed from sin and reborn as sons of God; we become members of Christ, are incorporated into the Church and made sharers in her mission: "Baptism is the sacrament of regeneration through water in the word."

No. 1257: The Lord himself affirms that Baptism is necessary for salvation. He also commands his disciples to proclaim the Gospel to all nations and to baptize them. Baptism is necessary for salvation for those to whom the Gospel has been proclaimed and who have had the possibility of asking for this Sacrament. The Church does not know of any means other than Baptism that assures entry into eternal beatitude; this is why she takes care not to neglect the mission she has received from the Lord to see that all who can be baptized are "reborn of water and the Spirit." *God has bound salvation to the sacrament of Baptism, but he himself is not bound by his sacraments.*

Confirmation

"And the Spirit of the Lord shall rest upon him, the spirit of wisdom and understanding, the spirit of counsel and might, the spirit of knowledge and the fear of the Lord" (Is. 11:2).

Baptism is the sacrament of spiritual birth: Confirmation is the sacrament of spiritual light, strength and perfection. Anyone who has been baptized is a candidate for Confirmation. The ordinary minister of Confirmation is a bishop[1] who places his hand on the candidate and anoints the forehead with holy oil mixed with balm in the shape of a cross, while saying the words "Be sealed with the Gift of the Holy Spirit", or as in the Eastern rites, "The seal of the gift that is the Holy Spirit." The oil signifies light and strength; the balm the sweet odour of sanctity.

Like Baptism, which it completes, Confirmation is given only once as it too imprints an indelible spiritual mark on the soul. This character perfects the baptismal priesthood of the faithful and fully equips one for the battle of professing faith in Christ publicly. It makes us *soldiers of Christ* by greatly increasing the life of sanctifying grace in our souls and leading us to live a more holy life undeterred by human respect or the "spirit of the world." Over and over again the Popes have urged the laity to be faithful to the grace of their Confirmation by living and acting as soldiers and apostles of Christ. According to Pope Pius XII, "By the chrism of Confirmation, the faithful are given added strength to protect and defend the Church, their mother, and the faith She has given them" (*Mystici Corporis*).

With sanctifying grace we also receive the seven gifts of the Holy Spirit. Given to us firstly in Baptism, these gifts are now received in a fuller and more perfect form to enable us to lead the life of a spiritual adult and perform the heroic deeds necessary for a life of sanctity. The seven gifts of the Holy Spirit are, viz., wisdom, understanding, counsel, fortitude, knowledge, piety and fear of the Lord (Is. 11:2). They increase

---

[1] In the East, ordinarily the Priest who baptizes also immediately confers Confirmation; in the West, this faculty may be conferred on a Priest only in exceptional circumstances.

our ability to receive actual grace which enables us to: (i) better appreciate the beauty and majesty of God; (ii) grasp the truths of the Faith; (iii) judge rightly what ought to be done in particular events for the sake of salvation; (iv) profess the Faith boldly, even unto death; (v) see God's likeness in all creatures; (vi) serve God with joy and look upon Him as our Father; and (vii) fear offending God and losing His love.

The Church, in the exercise of Her teaching authority, declares Confirmation to be a sacrament of Christ.[2] Christ established it while still on earth when he promised the Holy Spirit: "... it is to your advantage that I go away, for if I do not go away, the Counselor will not come to you; but if I go, I will send him to you" (Jn 16:7). From Scripture we see that Confirmation is a rite distinct from Baptism:

"Now when the apostles at Jerusalem heard that Samaria had received the word of God, they sent to them Peter and John, who came down and prayed for them that they might receive the Holy Spirit; for it had not yet fallen on any of them, but they had only been baptized in the name of the Lord Jesus. Then they laid their hands on them and they received the Holy Spirit" (Acts 8:14-17).

"On hearing this, they were baptized in the name of the Lord Jesus. And when Paul had laid his hands upon them, the Holy Spirit came on them; and they spoke with tongues and prophesied. There were about twelve of them in all" (Acts 19:5-7).

It is the Church's firm exhortation that although Confirmation is not absolutely necessary for salvation "the faithful are obliged to receive this Sacrament at the appropriate time."[3] Those who are dying and have not yet received Confirmation should do so in order that they may have a more glorious resurrection as soldiers of Christ. In the Western Church "the age of discretion" is taken as the reference point for receiving Confirmation; in the Eastern Rites, Confirmation is given to the children immediately after Baptism.[5] The Eastern practice highlights more the

---

[2] Council of Trent, *Canons on the Sacrament of Confirmation*, Canon 1, 3 March, 1547.
[3] *Code of Canon Law* #890.
[5] *Code of Canons of the Eastern Churches*, Canon #695.

unity of the sacraments of Christian initiation and is traceable directly to the first centuries of Christianity when Confirmation and Baptism comprised one single celebration, forming as it were a 'double sacrament.'

Each candidate for confirmation should have a *sponsor* who is a confirmed Catholic in good standing, desirably the same person who acted as sponsor in Baptism, at least sixteen years of age, and who is not either the father or mother of the candidate. The sponsor must personally touch the candidate during the ceremony by placing their right hand on the candidate's right shoulder. A spiritual relationship arises between the candidate and the sponsor from Confirmation that obliges the latter to do what he or she can to ensure that the candidate behaves as a true witness of Christ and faithfully fulfils the duties inherent in this sacrament.

Great care should be taken in preparing the candidate to receive Confirmation, endeavoring to ensure that he or she acquires an accurate knowledge of Christ, the workings of the Holy Spirit and the responsibilities of Christian life. Worthy reception of Confirmation should always be preceded by intense prayer, participation in the sacrament of Penance, and Holy Communion. The Apostles, when waiting for the descent of the Holy Spirit at Pentecost, spent nine days persevering together in prayer (Acts 1:14). Confirmation is our Pentecost.

The Fathers

St Theophilus of Antioch, *To Autolycus* 1, 12 (AD 181)
"Are you unwilling to be anointed with the oil of God? It is on this account that we are called Christians: because we are anointed with the oil of God."

Tertullian, *The Resurrection of the Dead* 8, 3 (inter AD 208-212)
"The flesh is anointed, so that the soul may be dedicated to holiness. The flesh is signed, so that the soul too may be fortified. The flesh is shaded by the imposition of hands, so that the soul too may be illuminated by the Spirit."

St Hippolytus of Rome, *The Apostolic Tradition* 22 (c. AD 215)
"The bishop, imposing his hands on them, shall make an invocation saying: 'O Lord God, who made them worthy of the remission of sins through the Holy Spirit's washing unto rebirth, send into them your grace so that they may serve you according to your will: for there is glory to you, to the Father and the Son with the Holy Spirit, in the Holy Church, both now and through the ages of ages, Amen.' Then, pouring the consecrated oil into his hands and imposing it on the head of the baptized, he shall say: 'I anoint you with holy oil in the Lord, the Father Almighty and Christ Jesus and the Holy Spirit.' And signing them on the forehead he shall kiss them and say: 'The Lord shall be with you.' And he that has been signed shall say: 'And with your spirit.' Thus shall he do with each."

St Cyprian of Carthage, *Letter to Jubaianus* 73, 9 (c. AD 254-256)
"For the reason, then, that they had already received legitimate and ecclesiastical Baptism, it was not necessary to baptize them again. Rather, that only which was lacking was done by Peter and John; and thus, prayer having been made over them, and hands having been imposed upon them, the Holy Spirit was invoked and was poured out upon them. This is even now the practice among us, so that those who are baptized in the Church are then brought to the prelates of the Church; and through our prayer and the imposition of hands, they receive the Holy Spirit and are perfected with the seal of the Lord."

The Council of Elvira, **Canon 77 (c. AD 300)**
"If a deacon, ruling a people without a bishop or presbyter, has baptized some of them, the bishop must bring them to the perfection of it through his blessing. But if they depart from this world beforehand: by reason of the faith in which he believed, he is able to be justified."

St Cyril of Jerusalem, *Catechetical Lectures* 21, 3 (c. AD 350)
"But beware of supposing that this is ordinary ointment ... Rather, it is a gracious gift of Christ; and it is made fit for the imparting of His Godhead by the coming of the Holy Spirit. This ointment is symbolically applied to your forehead and to your other senses; and while your body is anointed with the visible ointment, your soul is sanctified by the Holy and Lifecreating Spirit."

The Roman Catechism (1566)

Pt. II, Ch. III: First, it is necessary to teach that this Sacrament is not so necessary as to be utterly essential to salvation. Although not essential, however, it ought to be omitted by no one, but rather, on the contrary, in a matter so full of holiness through which the divine gifts are so liberally bestowed, the greater care should be taken to avoid all neglect. What God has proposed in common unto all for their sanctification, all should likewise most earnestly desire.

St Luke, indeed, describing this admirable effusion of the Holy Spirit, says: *And suddenly there came a sound from heaven, as of a mighty wind coming, and it filled the whole house, where they were sitting;* and a little after: *And they were all filled with the Holy Ghost.* From these words we may understand that, as that house was a type and figure of the Church, the Sacrament of Confirmation, which took its beginning from that day, appertains to all the faithful.

Catechism of the Catholic Church (1992)

No. 1302: It is evident from its celebration that the effect of the sacrament of Confirmation is the full outpouring of the Holy Spirit as once granted to the apostles on the day of Pentecost.

No. 1303: From the fact, Confirmation brings an increase and deepening of baptismal grace:

– it roots us more deeply in the divine filiation which makes us cry, "Abba! Father..."
– it unites us more firmly to Christ.
– it renders our bond with the Church more perfect.
– it gives us a special strength of the Holy Spirit to spread and defend the faith by word and action as true witnesses of Christ, to confess the name of Christ boldly, and never to be ashamed of the Cross.

No. 1304: Like Baptism which it completes, Confirmation is given only once, for it too imprints on the soul an *indelible spiritual mark*, the "character", which is the sign that Jesus Christ has marked a Christian with the seal of his Spirit by clothing him with power from on high so that he may be his witness.

No. 1305: The "character" perfects the common priesthood of the faithful, received in Baptism, and "the confirmed person receives the power to profess faith in Christ publicly and as it were officially (*quasi ex officio*)."

The Blessed Eucharist

"Truly, truly, I say to you, unless you eat the flesh of the Son of man and drink his blood, you have no life in you; 54 he who eats my flesh and drinks my blood has eternal life, and I will raise him up at the last day" (Jn 6:53-54).

The sacrament of the Blessed Eucharist is the Body, Blood, Soul and Divinity of Jesus Christ under the appearances, or accidents, of bread and wine. Unlike the other sacraments, it not only bestows grace, but contains the Author of Grace Himself. According to St Thomas Aquinas (S.T., III, q. 65 a. 3), all the other sacraments point to, or are servants of, the Blessed Eucharist.

Our Lord first promised the Eucharist in John 6:48-51:

"I am the bread of life. Your fathers ate the manna in the wilderness, and they died. This is the bread which comes down from heaven, that a man may eat of it and not die. I am the living bread which came down from heaven; if any one eats of this bread, he will live for ever; and the bread which I shall give for the life of the world is my flesh."

The Jews were scandalized and declared, "How can this man give us his flesh to eat?" (v. 52). Whenever His hearers misunderstood His meaning Christ always corrected them immediately by explaining clearly what He meant (e.g., Jn 3:3-6; Jn 11:14). On the other hand, whenever his hearers understood Him correctly but did not believe what He said He always repeated and stressed His statement:

"So Jesus said to them, 'Truly, truly, I say to you, unless you eat the flesh of the Son of man and drink his blood, you have no life in you; he who eats my flesh and drinks my blood has eternal life, and I will raise him up at the last day. For my flesh is food indeed, and my blood is drink indeed. He who eats my flesh and drinks my blood abides in me, and I in him. As the living Father sent me, and I live because of the Father, so he who eats me will live because of me. This is the bread which came down from heaven, not such as the fathers ate and died; he who eats this bread will live for ever'" (vv. 53-58).

The Jews then reacted by saying, "This is a hard saying; who can listen to it?" (v. 60) and "no longer went about with him" (v. 66). Christ let them go even though earlier He had said, "this is the will of him who sent me, that I should lose nothing of all that he has given me" (v. 39). Catholics, on the other hand, profess the faith of Simon Peter who answered "Lord, to whom can we go? You have the words of eternal life" (v. 68).

Christ fulfilled His promise to give us His Flesh and Blood at the Last Supper:

"Now as they were eating, Jesus took bread, and blessed, and broke it, and gave it to the disciples and said, 'Take, eat; this is my body.' And he took a cup, and when he had given thanks he gave it to them, saying, 'Drink of it, all of you; for this is my blood of the covenant, which is poured out for many for the forgiveness of sins'" (Mt 26:26-28; see also Mk 14:22-24; Lk 22:19-20; 1 Cor. 10:4-21).

Christ then commanded His Apostles to do what He had done: "Do this in remembrance of me" (Lk 22:19). The matter of the sacrament is bread and wine; the form, the words of consecration. It is understandable why Christ chose such basic foodstuffs for the matter to emphasize the Eucharist as food for our souls. As successors to the Apostles, the priests and bishops are the "ministers of consecration", consecrating the Eucharist at Mass. Upon pronouncing the respective consecratory prayers which climax with the words "This is my Body", "This is my Blood", the bread and wine become truly the Body and Blood of Christ.

The Church calls this mysterious change *Transubstantiation* (Lateran IV, 1215). The substances of the bread and the wine are changed respectively into the substances of Christ's Body and Blood, while the accidents (i.e., color, shape, taste, etc.) of the bread and the wine remain unchanged.

The priest is also normally the "minister of distribution", distributing the Eucharistic hosts to the faithful. Where necessary, lay "extraordinary ministers of the Eucharist" with due permission and authority may distribute the sacred species.

The priest celebrating Mass is obliged to receive the Eucharist under the two species of bread and wine. This is in order to properly fulfil the Rite as established by Our Lord. However, it is not obligatory for the laity to receive under both species since Christ's Body, Blood, Soul and Divinity are wholly present under either species through *concomitance* (from the Latin, accompanying as a companion). This is gathered from the words of St Paul: "Whoever, therefore, eats the bread or drinks the cup of the Lord in an unworthy manner will be guilty of profaning the body *and* blood of the Lord" (1 Cor. 11:27).

The Eucharist is the fruit of the Holy Sacrifice of the Mass which is the central act of worship of the Catholic Church. As defined by the Council of Trent, in the Mass "The same Christ who offered himself once in a bloody manner on the altar of the cross, is present and offered in an unbloody manner."[2] The Mass is therefore:

(i) A re-presentation of the Sacrifice of Calvary, making that same sacrifice present to Christians today.
(ii) A memorial of Christ's death, which is commemorated as a mystical reality.
(iii) A sacred banquet in which Christ gives Himself to the faithful as heavenly food.
(iv) An effective application of the merits gained by Christ on Calvary in proportion to the faith and charity of the faithful receiving the Eucharist.

Any person who has been validly baptized is a fit subject to receive the Eucharist. After reaching the age of reason and being properly instructed in the nature of the Eucharist, one is obliged to receive it at least once a year, at or about Easter time (Lateran IV, 1215). Our Lord Himself stated, "unless you eat the flesh of the Son of man and drink his blood, you have no life in you" (Jn 6:53). Since the time of Pope St Pius X (1903-14), all the faithful have been encouraged to communicate daily, as was the practice in the early Church.

In preparing for the reception of Holy Communion the candidate must first complete the prescribed fast of at least one-hour beforehand. The subject must in good conscience believe that he or she is in a state of grace, free from all mortal sin. Quoting St Paul again,

---

[2] Council of Trent, *Doctrine on the Sacrifice of the Mass*, Ch. 2, 17 Sept., 1562.

"Whoever, therefore, eats the bread or drinks the cup of the Lord in an unworthy manner will be guilty of profaning the body and blood of the Lord. For any one who eats and drinks without discerning the body eats and drinks judgment upon himself" (1 Cor. 11:27 & 29). A person in mortal sin must first go to confession and receive the sacrament of Penance before receiving the Eucharist. Furthermore, we should earnestly strive to free our souls of all venial sin, to increase as much as possible the inflow of grace.

After receiving communion, we should spend time in prayer making acts of faith, adoration and thanksgiving. According St Peter Julian Eymard, "the most solemn moment in Christian life is that of thanksgiving after Communion." In more recent times, Pope St John Paul II, echoing the words of the Second Vatican Council, has called the Eucharist the "source and summit of all Christian life." We should offer ourselves entirely to God and beg His graces for ourselves, others, the Church, and for the dead.

On each occasion we communicate worthily, we receive an increase of sanctifying grace, as well as sacramental grace, or claim to actual graces to help us live the life of holiness. Dwelling within us as long as the species of bread and wine remain, Christ's Soul is mysteriously united with our own, breathing into it His own love. Intimately united to Christ, we are thereby united to all the faithful as His Mystical Body: "... we who are many are one body, for we all partake of the one bread" (1 Cor. 10:17).

As food nourishes the body, so Holy Communion nourishes the soul by giving it new energy, fervor and vitality. It can preserve the soul from mortal sin by stifling our carnal appetites, weakening our sensual and worldly desires, and opening our eyes and minds to a love of those things of God, giving us a greater charity and willingness to follow Christ and His Church.

Being a living tabernacle of Christ on earth, the body too is given a special pledge: "he who eats my flesh and drinks my blood has eternal life, and I will raise him up at the last day" (Jn 6:54). It is fitting that the Christian body should not suffer permanent corruption, but share with Christ the privilege of a resurrection.

The Fathers

St Ignatius of Antioch, *Letter to the Philadelphians* 4, 1 (c. AD 110)
"Take care, then, to use one Eucharist, so that whatever you do, you do according to God: for there is one Flesh of Our Lord Jesus Christ, and one cup in the union of His Blood; one altar, as there is one bishop with the presbyters and my fellow servants, the deacons."

Tertullian, *The Crown* 3, 3 (AD 211)
"The Sacrament of the Eucharist, which the Lord commanded to be taken at meal times and by all, we take even before daybreak in congregations, but from the hand of none others except the presidents ... We take anxious care lest something of our Cup of Bread should fall upon the ground."

Origen, *Homilies on Numbers* Hom. 7, 2 (post AD 244)
"Formally, in an obscure way, there was manna for food; now, however, in full view, there is the true food, the flesh of the word of God, as He Himself says: 'My flesh is truly food, and My Blood is truly drink.'"

St Cyprian of Carthage, *The Lord's Prayer* 18 (AD 251-252)
"And we ask that this bread be given us daily, so that we who are in Christ and daily receive the Eucharist as the food of salvation, may not, by falling into some more grievous sin and then in abstaining from communicating, be withheld from the heavenly Bread, and be separated from Christ's Body."

St Ephrem of Edessa, *Homilies* 4, 4 (ante AD 373)
"And extending His hand, He gave them the Bread which His right hand had made holy: 'Take all of you eat of this, which my word has made holy. Do not now regard as bread that which I have given you; but take, eat this Bread, and do not scatter the crumbs; for what I have called My Body, that it is indeed. One particle from its crumbs is able to sanctify thousands and thousands, and is sufficient to afford life to those who eat of it. Take, eat, entertaining no doubt of faith, because this is My Body, and whoever eats it in belief eats in it Fire and Spirit."

St Ambrose of Milan, *Commentaries on Twelve of David's Psalms* 38, 25 (inter AD 381-397)
"We saw the Prince of Priests coming to us, we saw and heard Him offering His blood for us. We follow, inasmuch as we are able, being priests; and we offer the sacrifice on behalf of the people. And even if we are of but little merit, still, in the sacrifice, we are honorable. For even if Christ is not now seen as the one who offers the sacrifice, nevertheless it is He Himself that is offered in sacrifice here on earth when the Body of Christ is offered. Indeed, to offer Himself He is made visible to us, He whose word makes holy the sacrifice that is offered."

St Augustine of Hippo, *Letter to Bishop Boniface* 98, 9 (AD 408)
"Was not Christ immolated only once in His very Person? In the Sacrament, nevertheless, He is immolated for the people not only on every Easter Solemnity but on every day; and a man would not be lying if, when asked, he were to reply that Christ is being immolated. For if the Sacraments had not a likeness to those things of which they are Sacraments, they would not be Sacraments at all; and they generally take the names of those same things by reason of this likeness."

The Roman Catechism (1566)

Pt. II, Ch. IV: It must, therefore, be diligently explained what the Sacrament of the Eucharist signifies, that the faithful, beholding the sacred mysteries with their eyes, may also at the same time feed their souls with the contemplation of divine things. Three things, then, are signified by this Sacrament. The first is the Passion of Christ our Lord, a thing past; for He Himself said: *Do this for a commemoration of me,* and the Apostle says: *As often as you shall eat this bread, and drink the chalice, you shall show the death of the Lord, until he come.*

It is also significant of divine and heavenly grace, which is imparted at the present time by this Sacrament to nurture and preserve the soul. Just as in Baptism we are begotten unto newness of life and by Confirmation are strengthened to resist Satan and openly to profess the name of Christ, so by the Sacrament of the Eucharist are we nurtured and supported.

It is, thirdly, a foreshadowing of future eternal joy and glory, which, according to God's promises, we shall receive in our heavenly country.

Catechism of the Catholic Church (1992)

No. 1377: The Eucharistic presence of Christ begins at the moment of the consecration and endures as long as the Eucharistic species subsist. Christ is present whole and entire in each of the species and whole and entire in each of their parts, in such a way that the breaking of the bread does not divide Christ.

No. 1378: *Worship of the Eucharist.* In the liturgy of the Mass we express our faith in the real presence of Christ under the species of bread and wine by, among other ways, genuflecting or bowing deeply as a sign of adoration of the Lord. The Catholic Church has always offered and still offers to the sacrament of the Eucharist the cult of adoration, not only during Mass, but also outside of it, reserving the consecrated hosts with the utmost care, exposing them to the solemn veneration of the faithful, and carrying them in procession.

Penance

"'Peace be with you. As the Father has sent me, even so I send you.' And when he had said this, he breathed on them, and said to them, 'Receive the Holy Spirit. If you forgive the sins of any, they are forgiven; if you retain the sins of any, they are retained'" (Jn 20:21-23).

The sacrament of Penance is the sacrament by which sins committed after Baptism are remitted for those who confess them with true sorrow. As Baptism gives birth to the spiritual life, Penance resurrects it from the dead. The minister of the sacrament is one in Holy Orders, priest or bishop. The matter of Penance comprises all formal sins committed after Baptism as well as the penitent's contrition, confession and satisfaction; the form, the priest's words of absolution: "I absolve you from your sins in the name of the Father and of the Son and of the Holy Spirit." Any Christian who has committed mortal sin after Baptism is a fit subject for Penance.

The Church, in the exercise of Her teaching authority, declares Penance to be a sacrament instituted by Christ.[1] The external sign comprises the penitent's confession of sin, his act of contrition and the priest's absolution; and this sign produces grace, for no sin can be forgiven unless grace is infused into the soul. From Scripture, we see Christ directly bestowing the power to forgive sins on His Apostles (and their successors). After His resurrection, Christ appeared to them and said:

"'Peace be with you. As the Father has sent me, even so I send you.' And when he had said this, he breathed on them, and said to them, 'Receive the Holy Spirit. If you forgive the sins of any, they are forgiven; if you retain the sins of any, they are retained'" (Jn 20:21-23).

In this verse we see that Christ bestowed upon His Apostles the following: (i) mission (*"As the Father has sent me, even so I send you ..."*); (ii)

---

[1] Council of Trent, *Doctrine on the Sacrament of Penance*, Canon 1, 25 November, 1551.

power ("*Receive the Holy Spirit*"), and (iii) judgment as to when and how to exercise this power ("*If you forgive ...; if you retain.*"). This verse cannot be explained away by claiming that the Apostles were simply authorized to go out and preach forgiveness according to the following injunction: "that repentance and forgiveness of sins should be preached in his name to all nations" (Lk 24:47). If such were the case, John 20:21-23 would be utterly devoid of purpose.

Pope St John Paul II referred to John 20:23 as follows:

> Now this power to 'forgive sins' Jesus confers through the Holy Spirit upon ordinary men, themselves subject to the snare of sin, namely the Apostles ... This is one of the most awe-inspiring innovations of the Gospel! He confers this power on the Apostles also as something which they can transmit - as the Church has understood it from the beginning - to their successors, charged by the same Apostles with the mission and responsibility of continuing their work as proclaimers of the Gospel and ministers of Christ's redemptive work.[2]

Catholics are obliged by the legislation of the Church to receive the sacrament of Penance at least once a year (Lateran IV, 1215). For a valid reception of the sacrament the penitent must perform three acts: *Contrition*, *Confession* and *Satisfaction*.

Contrition is the primary and most essential condition for forgiveness. Without sorrow for sin there can be no possibility of pardon. Sorrow must be internal and genuine, not merely an outward show. It must be universal, that is, cover all mortal sins the penitent is aware of. The penitent must show a detestation of sin as a supreme evil, with an accompanying firm purpose of amendment to avoid it and all its occasions in the future.

Contrition for sin may be of two kinds: perfect and imperfect. Perfect contrition is sorrow for sin out of charity, or perfect love of God. Such contrition immediately reconciles the penitent to God. As Christ said, "her sins, which are many, are forgiven, for she loved much" (Lk

---

[2] Pope St John Paul II, *Reconciliatio et Paenitentia*, 1984, #29.

7:47). Nevertheless, reconciliation is not due to perfect contrition alone but must include a desire of receiving sacramental Penance.

Imperfect contrition, or attrition, is sorrow for sin based on less perfect motives such as fear of hell, loss of heaven or the horror and ugliness of sin. Even so, attrition is still regarded as true sorrow and pleasing to God.

When confessing, the penitent must declare to the priest all mortal sins they can sincerely remember. The precise nature of the offense must be related, not merely a generic reference, e.g., "I attempted to attack my neighbor with a knife", not "I tried to hurt my neighbor." The exact number of times each sin has been committed must also be given. It is important to note that where a penitent has genuinely forgotten to confess a particular sin, or sins, they are still forgiven, being included in the words, "for these and all my sins, I am very sorry." Their guilt does not return; our only obligation is to confess them if remembered at the next confession. Nor is the penitent obliged to confess where he possesses a serious doubt as to whether the sin was mortal or not as full advertence is required to commit a formal mortal sin.

It is always good and proper to confess all venial sins and faults committed in the sacrament of Penance. The advantage of this practice lies in the added sanctifying and sacramental grace the penitent receives to avoid future venial sins, as well as a total or partial remission of the debt of temporal punishment.

Satisfaction is the voluntary acceptance by the penitent of the penance given by the priest. Normally, satisfaction would take the form of prayers or acts of charity or other good works. Their aim is to remit, in whole or in part, the debt of temporal punishment that often remains after the sin has been forgiven. Any person who, during confession, has no intention to make the satisfaction imposed, fails to receive the sacrament validly.

Besides the wonderful spiritual benefits for the soul, the sacrament of Penance can also give to penitents genuine peace of mind. Experience testifies as to how many of the mental difficulties that arise from great guilt or fear of death and judgment, are prevented or eradicated by frequent confession. Ideally, Penance is also an excellent means of obtaining sound spiritual advice from one experienced in the direction of souls.

The Fathers

St Ignatius of Antioch, *Letter to the Philadelphians* 8, 1 (c. AD 110)
"I did my best as a man devoted to unity. But where there is division and anger, God does not dwell. The Lord, however, forgives all who repent, if their repentance leads to the unity of God and to the council of the bishop. I have faith in the grace of Jesus Christ; and He will remove from you every chain."

St Cyprian of Carthage, *The Lapsed* 29 (AD 251)
"I beseech you, brethren, let everyone who has sinned confess his sin while he is still in this world, while his confession is still admissible, while satisfaction and remission made through the priests are pleasing before the Lord."

St Cyprian of Carthage, *Letter to Fidus* 64 (59), 1 (AD 251-252)
"Still, we did not think that peace once granted in whatever way by a priest of God should be taken away; and for this reason we have allowed Victor to avail himself of the communion granted."

Firmilian of Caesarea, *Letter to Cyprian* 75, 16 (AD 255-256)
"'Receive the Holy Spirit: if you forgive any man his sins, they shall be forgiven, and if you retain any man's sins, they shall be retained.' Therefore, the power of forgiving sins was given to the Apostles and to the Churches which these men, sent by Christ, established; and to the bishops who succeed them by being ordained in their place."

St Pacian of Barcelona, *Letters to Sympronian* 1, 6 (inter AD 375-392)
"God never threatens the repentant, rather He pardons the penitent. You will say that it is God alone who can do this. True enough, but it is likewise true that He does it through his priests, who exercise His power."

St Augustine of Hippo, *Homilies on the Epistles of John* 1, 6 (AD 416)
"Before all confession, lest anyone suppose himself just, and in the eyes of God, who sees things as they are, a man who did not exist and who now does exist is lifting up his neck in pride - before all, therefore, there is confession; then there is love, for what is it that is said about love? 'Love covers over a multitude of sins.'"

The Roman Catechism (1566)

Pt. II, Ch. V: Hence the Council of Trent declares: *For those who fall into sin after Baptism the sacrament of Penance is as necessary to salvation as is Baptism for those who have not been already baptized.* The saying of St Jerome that Penance is *a second plank*, is universally known and highly commended by all subsequent writers on sacred things. As he who suffers shipwreck has no hope of safety, unless, perchance, he seize on some plank from the wreck, so he that suffers the shipwreck of baptismal innocence, unless he cling to the saving plank of Penance, has doubtless lost all hope of salvation.

Catechism of the Catholic Church (1992)

No. 1461: Since Christ entrusted to his apostles the ministry of reconciliation, bishops who are their successors, and priests, the bishop's collaborators, continue to exercise this ministry. Indeed bishops and priests, by virtue of the sacrament of Holy Orders, have the power to forgive all sins "in the name of the Father, and of the Son, and of the Holy Spirit."

No. 1468: "The whole power of the sacrament of Penance consists in restoring us to God's grace and joining us with him in an intimate friendship." Reconciliation with God is thus the purpose and effect of this sacrament. For those who receive the sacrament of Penance with contrite heart and religious disposition, reconciliation is usually followed by peace and serenity of conscience with strong spiritual consolation ...

Anointing of the Sick

"Is any among you sick? Let him call for the elders of the church, and let them pray over him, anointing him with oil in the name of the Lord; and the prayer of faith will save the sick man, and the Lord will raise him up; and if he has committed sins, he will be forgiven" (Js. 5:14-15).

Anointing of the Sick is the sacrament applied to those in danger of death from bodily illness or physical infirmity. Its effects can be threefold: firstly, the grace of God is bestowed for the recipient's spiritual strength and consolation; secondly, the forgiveness of the recipient's sins; and thirdly, if it is God's will, the recipient may be restored to physical health.

The Church teaches solemnly that Anointing of the Sick is a sacrament instituted by Christ.[1] It is a sensible sign having for its matter anointing with olive oil. The bishop on Holy Thursday blesses this oil. The sacrament's form comprises the following words: "Through this holy anointing may the Lord in His love and mercy help you with the grace of the Holy Spirit. May the Lord who frees you from sin save you and raise you up." Furthermore, it is an efficacious sign of grace for it gives the recipient supernatural solace and strength, while at the same time forgiving whatever sins he may have.

The minister of the sacrament is a priest or bishop. Formerly, the priest conferred the sacrament by individually anointing the five sense organs while pronouncing each time the prescribed words. It was always recognized, however, that a single unction sufficed for the sacrament's validity. Today, the recipient's forehead and hands may be anointed with holy oil only once.

From Scripture, we see the sacrament mentioned explicitly by St James:

---

[1] Council of Trent, *Doctrine on the Sacrament of Extreme Unction*, Canon 1, 25 November, 1551.

"Is any among you sick? Let him call for the elders of the church, and let them pray over him, anointing him with oil in the name of the Lord; and the prayer of faith will save the sick man, and the Lord will raise him up; and if he has committed sins, he will be forgiven" (Js. 5:14-15).

It was also prefigured during Our Lord's public ministry:

"So they went out and preached that men should repent. And they cast out many demons, and anointed with oil many that were sick and healed them" (Mk 6:12-13).

As the primary purpose of the Anointing of the Sick is to spiritually strengthen the soul weakened by sin and subject to temptation, it is not administered to anyone not having attained the use of reason and thus incapable of committing sin. Furthermore, "danger of death" does not mean "risk of imminent death." Hence, soldiers about to do battle, or prisoners on death row, are not valid candidates for this sacrament. The sacrament of Penance meets their needs.

To receive Anointing of the Sick fruitfully, the recipient must be in a state of grace. In cases where the recipient is not, confession must be made beforehand. Where the recipient is unconscious and unable to make a confession, attrition is sufficient for the sacrament to restore him to sanctifying grace. However, without at least attrition, the sacrament will have no effect.

When fruitfully received, Anointing of the Sick gives an increase in sanctifying grace and, through actual grace, enables the recipient to endure more easily the sufferings and pains of sickness, and to resist with greater fortitude the last attacks of the devil. The soul of the sick one is filled with supernatural courage, a divine peace and a holy resignation enabling him to meet death with a disposition similar to that of Our Lord on the Cross. All mortal and venial sins are remitted; the *Apostolic Blessing* given in conjunction with the sacrament remits the debt of temporal punishment due to sin.

In the prayers accompanying the sacrament, God is invoked to heal the sick person. These prayers have a particular sacramental efficacy, without actually appealing for a miracle. Rather, what is sought is a special aid, and stimulus of the patient's natural recuperative powers.

However, restoration of the patient's health will only be forthcoming if "it is expedient for the soul's salvation."[2]

Catholics should be instructed against an unreasonable delay in calling a priest to administer Anointing of the Sick to their loved ones. In the first place it is a sacrament for the sick, not only for the dying. It should be administered whenever there is a serious danger of death even if it is more likely that the recipient will recover. An early reception of the sacrament also increases the likelihood of a physical recovery. Finally, if the sacrament is administered while the recipient still has full use of his faculties he can properly prepare for and receive it with more favorable dispositions.

The Fathers

Origen, *Homilies on Leviticus* Hom. 2, 4 (post AD 244)

"In addition to these there is also a seventh, albeit hard and laborious: the remission of sins through penance, when the sinner washes his pillow with tears, when his tears are day and night his nourishment, and when he does not shrink from declaring his sin to a priest of the Lord and from seeking medicine, after the manner of him who says, 'I said, to the Lord I will accuse myself of my iniquity, and you forgave the disloyalty of my heart.' In this way there is fulfilled that too, which the Apostle James says: 'If, then, there is anyone sick, let him call the presbyters of the Church, and let them impose hands upon him, anointing him with oil in the name of the Lord; and the prayer of faith will save the sick man, and if he be in sins, they shall be forgiven him.'"

Aphraates the Persian Sage, *Treatises* 23, 3 (inter AD 336-345)

"But a gate has been opened for seeking peace, whereby the mist has lifted from the reason of the multitude; and light has dawned in the mind; and from the glistening olive, fruits are put forth, in which there is a sign of the sacrament of life, by which Christians are perfected, as well as priests and kings and prophets. It illuminates the darkness, anoints the sick, and leads back penitents in its secret sacrament."

---

[2] Council of Trent, *Ibid.*, Chapter 2.

St John Chrysostom, *The Priesthood* 3, 5, 195 (AD 387)
"The latter often save the sick and perishing soul - sometimes by imposing a lighter penance, sometimes by preventing the fall. Priests accomplish this not only by teaching and admonishing, but also by the help of prayer. Not only at the time of our regeneration (in baptism), but even afterward, they have authority to forgive sins. 'Is there anyone among you sick? Let him call in the priests of the church, and let them pray over him, anointing him with oil in the name of the Lord. And the prayer of faith shall save the sick man, and the Lord shall raise him up, and if he have committed sins, he shall be forgiven.'"

Pope St Innocent I, *Letter to Decentius* 25, 8, 11 (AD 416)
"There is no doubt that this is to be taken or understood in regard to the sick faithful, who are able to be anointed with the holy oil of chrism, which, having been confected by a bishop, is permitted not only to priests but also to all as Christians, for anointing in case of their own necessity or in that of their people."

St Cyril of Alexandria, *Worship and Adoration in Spirit and in Truth* 6 (inter AD 412-429)
"But you, if some part of your body is suffering, and you really believe that saying the words 'Lord Sabaoth!' or some such appellation which divine Scripture attributes to God in respect to this nature has the power to drive that evil from you, go ahead and pronounce those words, making them a prayer for yourself ... I recall also the saying in the divinely inspired Scripture: 'Is anyone among you ill? Let him call in the Presbyters of the Church ... and if he be in sins they shall be forgiven him.'"

St Caesarius of Arles, *Sermons* 13 (265), 3 (ante AD 542)
"As often as some infirmity overtakes a man, let him who is ill receive the Body and Blood of Christ; let him humbly and in faith ask the presbyters for blessed oil, to anoint his body, so that what was written may be fulfilled in him; 'Is anyone among you sick ...?' See to it, brethren, that whoever is ill hasten to the church, both that he may receive health of body and will merit to obtain the forgiveness of his sins."

The Roman Catechism (1566)

Pt. II, Ch. VI: Having thus proved that Extreme Unction is truly and properly to be numbered among the Sacraments, we rightly infer that it owes its institution to Christ our Lord. It was subsequently made known and promulgated to the faithful by the Apostle St James.

Our Savior Himself, however, seems to have given some indication of it, when He sent His disciples two and two before Him; for the Evangelist informs us that *going forth, they preached that all should do penance; and they cast out many Devils, and anointed with oil many who were sick, and healed them.*

Catechism of the Catholic Church (1992)

No. 1511: The Church believes and confesses that among the seven sacraments there is one especially intended to strengthen those who are being tried by illness, the Anointing of the Sick:

> This sacred anointing of the sick was instituted by Christ Our Lord as a true and proper sacrament of the New Testament. It is alleged to indeed by Mark, but is recommended to the faithful and promulgated by James the apostle and brother of the Lord.

No. 1514: The Anointing of the Sick "is not a sacrament for those only who are at the point of death. Hence, as soon as anyone of the faithful begins to be in danger of death from sickness or old age, the fitting time for him to receive this sacrament has certainly already arrived."

Holy Orders

"Hence I remind you to rekindle the gift of God that is within you through the laying on of my hands ..." (2 Tim. 1:6).

The sacrament of Holy Orders is that sacrament which imparts to man the gift of the Holy Spirit to worthily perform the holy functions of deacon, priest or bishop. One in Orders is a mediator between God and men, offering the homage of the faithful to God and, in return, bringing down from God to them His graces and blessings. At the Last Supper Christ consecrated bread and wine into His Body and Blood and then told His Apostles to "Do this in remembrance of me" (Lk 22:19). By these words Christ ordained them priests to offer the sacrifice of the Mass and act as "stewards of the mysteries of God" (1 Cor. 4:1), including forgiving the sins of others (Jn 20:23).

The matter of the sacrament of Orders is the imposition of hands made by the bishop; the form the various solemn words of consecration found in the Rites of Ordination for deacon, priest and bishop invoking God to bestow on the ordinand the graces of the Holy Spirit related to each ministry. Orders bestows:

(i) The sacramental Character, the indelible mark on the soul with gives the power for the exercise of the order conferred.
(ii) Sanctifying grace.
(iii) Sacramental grace and special actual graces needed for the worthy discharge of the sacred functions.

Any baptized male is an eligible candidate for Holy Orders. This is a law not of the Church's own making but, as successive Popes have reaffirmed in recent decades, one given to Her by Our Lord Jesus Christ Himself and therefore cannot be altered:

> She (the Catholic Church) holds that it is not admissible to ordain women to the priesthood, for very fundamental reasons. These reasons include: the example recorded in the Sacred Scriptures of Christ choosing his Apostles only from among men; the constant

practice of the Church, which has imitated Christ in choosing only men; and her living teaching authority which has consistently held that the exclusion of women from the priesthood is in accordance with God's plan for his Church.[1]

Wherefore, in order that all doubt may be removed regarding a matter of great importance, a matter which pertains to the Church's divine constitution itself, in virtue of my ministry of confirming the brethren (cf. Lk 22:32) we declare that the Church has no authority whatsoever to confer priestly ordination on women and that this judgment is to be held definitively by all the faithful.[2]

The Church, in the exercise of Her teaching authority, declares Holy Orders to be a sacrament instituted by Christ.[3] From Scripture, it is clear that by a visible rite the Apostles, through prayer and the laying of hands, ordained assistants and successors:

"Therefore, brethren, pick out from among you seven men of good repute, full of the Spirit and of wisdom, whom we may appoint to this duty ... These they set before the apostles, and they prayed and laid their hands upon them" (Acts 6:3-6).

"While they were worshiping the Lord and fasting, the Holy Spirit said, 'Set apart for me Barnabas and Saul for the work to which I have called them.' Then after fasting and praying they laid their hands on them and sent them off" (Acts 13:2-4).

"And when they had appointed elders for them in every church, with prayer and fasting they committed them to the Lord in whom they believed ..." (Acts 14:23).

(St Paul to St Timothy) *"I remind you to rekindle the gift of God that is within you through the laying on of my hands ..."* (2 Tim. 1:6).

---

[1] Pope Paul VI, *Response to the Letter of Dr F. D. Coggan, Archbishop of Canterbury, concerning the Ordination of Women to the Priesthood*, 30 November, 1975.
[2] Pope St John Paul II, Apostolic Epistle, *Ordinatio Sacerdotalis*, 22 May, 1994, #4.
[3] Council of Trent, *Canons on the Sacrament of Order*, Canon 3, 15 July, 1563.

(St Paul to Titus) *"This is why I left you in Crete, that you might amend what was defective, and appoint elders in every town as I directed you"* (Tit. 1:5).[4]

The deacon receives power to effectively preach the Gospel and worthily assist the priest and bishop at Mass. He may also baptize, distribute Holy Communion, perform marriages, preside over funerals and administer parishes beside the priest in the service of the bishop. Since the Second Vatican Council the diaconate as a permanent state, while always being maintained in the East, has been restored in the Latin Rite and can be conferred on married men.

The priest is made "another Christ", receiving the power to sanctify and save souls through the sacrifice of the Mass and by forgiving sins. The priest in carrying out these functions is so united to Christ that the consecration or absolution is produced by both. That is, Christ is the principal cause, and the priest, however unworthy, his instrument. The priest is a co-worker with the bishop and his ministry is performed in the bishop's name. By virtue of the sacramental grace, the priest is given a special habit of love to work for the salvation of souls, a special habit of apostolate to work with zeal for them, and a special habit of sacrifice to be ever willing to sacrifice himself as a spiritual father for the supernatural benefit of others.

The bishop in his ordination receives the full plenitude of the priesthood, receiving also the power of confirming and ordaining, and is thus a successor of the Apostles. The episcopate is not a sacrament distinct from the priesthood, but rather its full expression. A bishop has authority to teach and guarantee the continuity of the Catholic Faith, decide on questions relating to faith and morals, to confirm, consecrate and ordain, subject to the Holy See.

In spiritual power, the priesthood incorporates the diaconate, the episcopate incorporates the priesthood and diaconate. All three degrees were possessed by the Apostles and later, in accordance with the direction of Christ, were passed on by them, wholly or in part, to others as the requirements of the growing Church dictated. The Church must always

---

[4] The Catholic priesthood is identical with this office of elder. In fact, the word 'priest' is simply an abbreviated English rendering of the Latin transliteration (presbyter) of the Greek word for elder - *presbuteros*.

possess bishops, but, strictly speaking, need not always have priests or deacons.

The bishops of the world together with the Pope form the *Hierarchy of Jurisdiction*. The Pope is the successor to St Peter, the Bishops the other Apostles: *"the Holy Spirit has made you overseers, to care for the church of the Lord"* (Acts 20:28). The Pope's jurisdiction covers the entire Church: that of a bishop, over a particular diocese and its members. The bishops together with the Pope also form the *Teaching Church*. When assembled under Papal authority to issue solemn decrees in General Council or, when dispersed, but united with the Pope in teaching that a doctrine forms part of the Deposit of Faith, they are infallible.

The discipline of clerical celibacy is of ecclesiastical rather than divine origin. It was only introduced as a mandatory rule in the Western Church during the eleventh century, while in the East married men have always been allowed to become priests. However, once ordained, an Eastern Rite priest cannot marry, and only celibates can be chosen as bishops. The state of celibacy for the sake of the Kingdom of heaven is an inherently higher state than marriage and is overtly praised as so by Our Lord and St Paul:

"Not all men can receive this saying, but only those to whom it is given. For there are eunuchs who have been so from birth, and there are eunuchs who have been made eunuchs by men, and there are eunuchs who have made themselves eunuchs for the sake of the kingdom of heaven. He who is able to receive this, let him receive it" (Mt 19:11-12; cf.1 Cor. 7:32; Rev. 14:4).

The Church also lays the obligation of celibacy on Her clergy in order that they may serve God with an undivided heart, undistracted by family affections and cares. The Second Vatican Council recognized this in the following terms:

> Let them perceive as well the superiority of virginity consecrated to Christ, so that by a choice which is maturely thought out and magnanimous they may attach themselves to God by a total gift of body and soul.[5]

---

[5] Second Vatican Council, *Decree on Priestly Formation*, 1965, #10.

The Fathers

St Clement of Rome, *Letter to the Corinthians* 40, 5 (c. AD 96)
"To the high priest, indeed, proper ministrations are allotted, to the priests a proper place is appointed, and upon the levites their proper services are imposed. The layman is bound by the ordinances for the laity."

St Ignatius of Antioch, *Letter to the Trallians* 2, 2 (c. AD 110)
"It is necessary, therefore, - and such is your practice - that you do nothing without the bishop, and that you be subject also to the presbytery, as to the Apostles of Jesus Christ our hope, in whom we shall be found, if we live in Him. It is necessary also that the deacons, the dispensers of the mysteries of Jesus Christ, be in every way pleasing to all men. For they are not the deacons of food and drink, but servants of the Church of God ... In like manner let everyone respect the deacons as they would respect Jesus Christ, and just as they respect the bishop as a type of the Father, and the presbyters as the council of God and college of Apostles. Without these, it cannot be called a Church ..."

St Ignatius of Antioch, *Letter to the Smyrnaeans* 8, 1 (c. AD 110)
"You must all follow the bishop as Jesus Christ follows the Father, and the presbytery as you would the Apostles. Reverence the deacons as you would the command of God. Let no one do anything of concern to the Church without the bishop. Let that be considered a valid Eucharist which is celebrated by the bishop, or by one whom he appoints. Wherever the bishop appears, let the people be there; just as wherever Jesus Christ is, there is the Catholic Church. Nor is it permitted without the bishop either to baptize or to celebrate the agape; but whatever he approve, this too is pleasing to God, so that whatever is done will be secure and valid."

St Hippolytus of Rome, *The Apostolic Tradition* 2 (c. AD 215)
"Let the bishop be ordained after he has been chosen by all the people. When someone pleasing to all has been named, let the people assemble on the Lord's Day with the presbyters and with such bishops as may be present. All giving assent, the bishops shall impose hands on him, and the

presbytery shall stand by in silence. Indeed, all shall remain silent, praying in their hearts for the descent of the Spirit."

St Cyprian of Carthage, *Letter to Certain Clergy and Laity of Spain* **67 (68) 5 (AD 256)**
"For the proper celebrating of ordinations all the neighboring bishops of the same province should assemble with that people for whom a prelate is being ordained ... And we see that this was done by you in the ordination of our colleague Sabinus, so that the episcopate was conferred upon him and hands were imposed."

St Gregory of Nyssa, *Sermon on the Baptism of Christ* **(c. AD 383)**
"This same power of the word also makes the priest venerable and honorable, separated from the generality of men by the new blessing bestowed upon him. Yesterday he was but one of the multitude, one of the people; suddenly he is made a guide, a president, a teacher of piety, an instructor in hidden mysteries."

St Jerome, *Letter to Pammachius* **48, 21 (c. AD 393)**
"Those persons chosen to be bishops, presbyters, or deacons are either virgins or widowers; or certainly, having once received the priesthood, they remain forever chaste."

The Roman Catechism (1566)

Pt. II, Ch. VII: The power of orders not only embraces the power of consecrating the Eucharist, but also fits and prepares the souls of men for its reception. It also embraces all else that can have any reference to the Eucharist. Regarding this power numerous passages of Sacred Scripture may be adduced; but the weightiest and most striking are those which are read in St John and St Matthew: *As the Father,* says our Lord, *hath sent me I also send you ... Receive ye the Holy Ghost; whose sins you shall forgive they are forgiven them, and whose sins you shall retain they are retained*; and: *Amen, I say to you, whatsoever you shall bind upon earth shall be bound also in heaven; and whatsoever you shall loose upon earth shall be loosed also in heaven.*

Catechism of the Catholic Church (1992)

No. 1545: The redemptive sacrifice of Christ is unique, accomplished once for all; yet it is made present in the Eucharistic sacrifice of the Church. The same is true of the one priesthood of Christ; it is made present through the ministerial priesthood without diminishing the uniqueness of Christ's priesthood: "Only Christ is the true priest, the others being only his ministers."

No. 1554: "The divinely instituted ecclesiastical ministry is exercised in different degrees by those who even from ancient times have been called bishops, priests and deacons." Catholic doctrine, expressed in the liturgy, the Magisterium and the constant practice of the Church, recognizes that there are two degrees of ministerial participation in the priesthood of Christ: the episcopacy and the presbyterate. The diaconate is intended to help and serve them. For this reason the term sacerdos in current usage denotes bishops and priests but not deacons. Yet Catholic doctrine teaches that degrees of priestly participation (episcopate and presbyterate) and the degree of service (diaconate) are all three conferred by a sacramental act called "ordination", that is, by the sacrament of Holy Orders ...

No. 1584: Since it is ultimately Christ who acts and effects salvation through the ordained minister, the unworthiness of the latter does not prevent Christ from acting. St Augustine states this forcefully:

> "As for the proud minister he is to be ranked with the Devil. Christ's gift is not thereby profaned: what flows through him keeps its purity, and what passes through him remains clear and reaches the fertile earth ... The spiritual power of the sacrament is indeed comparable to light: Those to be enlightened receive it in its purity, and if it should pass through defiled beings, it is not itself defiled" (*In Jo. ev.* 5, 15).

Holy Matrimony

"What therefore God has joined together, let not man put asunder" (Mt 19:6).

The sacrament of Holy Matrimony is the sacrament that unites a Christian man and woman as husband and wife in an intimate community of life and love under a sacred covenant until death. Between baptized persons, marriage is always a sacrament; between unbaptized persons it is a natural contract.

The ministers of the sacrament of Holy Matrimony are the marrying couple themselves through the mutual giving and acceptance of the marriage vows. Their consent to marry each other constitutes the matter and form of the sacrament. The marrying couple are, therefore, also the subjects of the sacrament. Consequently, the priest who officiates at the marriage is not its minister, but instead attends as the Church's official representative to ensure that all necessary requirements are carried out, to offer Mass or prayers for the couple and to bless their union.

The Church desires that those who receive the sacrament of Holy Matrimony do so in a state of grace. Worthy reception gives (i) an increase of sanctifying grace and (ii) through the *marital bond*, the actual graces and gifts necessary to carry out the duties of the married state. The marital bond formed by the sacrament makes them a living image of Christ and the Church, and urges them to imitate this relationship in their own lives. It thus guarantees all the assistance necessary for the couple to live a life together of peace and love and to overcome all obstacles until death.

Holy Matrimony imposes serious obligations upon the husband and wife. The husband is obliged to render support and protection to his wife, while the wife should love and reverence her husband as her head: "Wives, be subject to your husbands, as to the Lord. For the husband is the head of the wife as Christ is the head of the church, his body, and is himself its Savior. As the church is subject to Christ, so let wives also be subject in everything to their husbands" (Eph. 5:22-24). Both husband and wife are mutually bound to live together and show marital affection:

"Husbands, love your wives" (Eph. 5:25); "train the young women to love their husbands" (Tit. 2:4).

As parents, the husband and wife are bound to provide all that is necessary for the proper upbringing of their children. The great endeavor of parents should be to raise their children for God, as they hold the place of God in their families. Parents must preserve their children in life and health, instruct and correct them, set them a good example, pray for them, and have them properly educated in the Faith: "Fathers ... bring them up in the discipline and instruction of the Lord" (Eph. 6:4); "The rod and reproof give wisdom, but a child left to himself brings shame to his mother" (Prov. 29:15).

According to the teaching of the Church, Holy Matrimony has various purposes: the procreation and education of children; mutual help and companionship; and sanctification of the spouses:

> Not only was marriage intended for the propagation of the human race, but also that the lives of husband and wife might be better and happier.[1]

> By their very nature, the institution of matrimony itself and conjugal love are ordained for the procreation and education of children, and find in them their ultimate crown.[2]

> Christian spouses have a special sacrament by which they are fortified and consecrated as it were in the duties and dignity of their state. By virtue of this sacrament, as they fulfill their conjugal and family mission, they are imbued with the spirit of Christ.[3]

God created man and woman to *complement* each other, each one possessing in qualities and needs what the other lacks. Each partner finds in marriage greater happiness and contentment, and realizes, as it were, a greater and more complete fullness of life. Through the marital act the couple express their mutual and unselfish love for each other. For Christians, this love is elevated to a supernatural level in which the husband and wife love each other in God and for God, reflecting the love

---

[1] Pope Leo XIII, *Arcanum Divinae* 1880, #26.
[2] Second Vatican Council, *Gaudium et Spes*, #48.
[3] *Ibid.*

that exists between Christ and His Church.

Because procreation is an essential of marriage, couples who use contraceptives to deliberately avoid conception consequently frustrate God's purpose for marriage and are guilty of grave sin (Pope Pius XI, *Casti Connubii* 1930; Pope Paul VI, *Humanae Vitae* 1968; Pope St John Paul II, *Veritatis Splendor* 1993; *Evangelium Vitae* 1995). The conjugal act gives human beings a share in God's creative power. Hence, for a couple to deliberately frustrate the conception of children is tantamount to dictating to God when He will create a life destined for eternal fellowship with Him in heaven.

The Christian ideal of marriage can be expressed in the following short formula: *"One with one to the exclusion of all others until death."* Hence, Christian marriage possesses:

(i) *Strict Unity*: Christian marriage excludes *Polygamy*, where a man has more than one wife; and *Polyandry*, where a woman has more than one husband.

(ii) *Perpetual Stability*: This excludes all possibility of divorce. Sacramental marriage is unbreakable by any human power: "What therefore God has joined together, let not man put asunder" (Mt 19:6; cf. Mk 10:11-12; Lk 16:18; 1 Cor. 7:2-11). Divorce is contrary to the good of the offspring, destroys utterly the last vestiges of love and companionship between the husband and wife, and opens the floodgates to immorality.

> Thus, being firmly established by the Lord, the unity of marriage is founded on the equal personal dignity of husband and wife ... and God wills the indissolubility of marriage as a fruit and a sign of the absolutely faithful love that God has for man and that the Lord Jesus has for the Church.[4]

(iii) *Perfect and Permanent Fidelity*: This obligation binds both partners equally. Both Christian teaching and the natural law forbid infidelity to matrimonial obligations in either the husband or the wife.

---

[4] Pope St John Paul II, *Familiaris Consortio* 1981, #20.

The Church permits a *separation* of husband and wife in certain cases (e.g., cruelty, adultery, anti-Catholic activity, apostasy, living a criminal and disreputable life), but cannot permit either to marry again during the lifetime of the other. Permission to separate is obtained from the local Bishop, but one may leave upon one's own authority if there is danger in delay (Canon 1153). In all these cases, however, if the evil ceases, married life must be resumed. To separate from one's lawful spouse for good reason is no sin; sometimes it is a moral necessity.

The State has no power to dissolve the marriage bond *even between non-Catholics, whether baptised or unbaptised*. After a separation of husband and wife, the parties may go through a form of so-called divorce, to secure one's rights to property, maintenance, and the custody of the children. A separated or divorced person is not free to start dating another. Such conduct is a source both of temptation and of scandal. A separated or deserted spouse who remains faithful is a very important witness to Christ and Christian marriage.[5]

Only where the *Pauline Privilege* operates is separation and remarriage allowed. In the case where one member of an unbaptized couple converts and is baptized, and the other partner inhibits the practice of the convert's faith, the baptized partner is free to leave the unbaptized spouse and marry again (1 Cor. 7:12-15; Canons 1143-1147).

Annulments are distinguishable from dissolution of marriage in that they are pronouncements by the Church that there *never existed a valid marriage in the first place*. To be declared null, it must be ascertained that some essential element was absent at the time of marriage. Grounds for annulment include, for example: psychological incapacity; consent extracted through force or fear; deceit or fraud perpetrated to secure consent; an intention to have no children; an intention to exclude fidelity or permanence.

The parties to a marriage covenant are a baptized man and woman free to marry, i.e., not impeded by any natural or Church law. Impediments, or obstacles to marriage, make a person incapable of validly entering marriage. For a marriage to be valid, *both* parties must be free of impediments. Some of the more important impediments are:

---

[5] Cf. *Apologetics and Catholic Doctrine*, Archbishop M. Sheehan, The Saint Austin Press, London, rev. ed. 2001, pp. 602-603.

- *Age*: The Church sets a minimum age for a man and a woman to marry.
- *Existing marriage*: A person already bound by an existing marriage tie cannot marry again.
- *Consanguinity* (relationship by blood): Close blood relations cannot marry validly. For example, uncle and niece. Marriage between first cousins requires a dispensation from the bishop.
- *Disparity of religion*: A Catholic cannot validly marry an unbaptised person unless the Bishop grants a dispensation.
- *Crime*: One who kills one's own or another's spouse, with a view to marrying a particular person, cannot validly enter that marriage.
- *Impotence*: If, before marriage, the man or the woman certainly suffers from permanent impotence, no marriage can take place.
- *Holy Orders and vows of chastity*: A deacon, priest, or bishop, or a religious man or woman who has taken a public vow of perpetual chastity, cannot validly marry while bound by that vow.

The Church, for weighty reasons, can grant a dispensation from *some* of the above impediments. In some cases, the Church will refuse a dispensation – for the spiritual good of her members. If no dispensation is obtained, the marriage is invalid, that is, *null and void*. Where the impediment is based on divine law (e.g., a pre-existing marriage), the Church can grant no dispensation.

In order to discover impediments, the Church has had the custom of publishing *Marriage Banns*. Banns have a three-fold purpose:

(i) they give people the opportunity to disclose impediments that might otherwise remain unknown;
(ii) prevent secret marriages;
(iii) give parents the opportunity to intervene if necessary.

All Catholics desiring to marry are bound to exchange their vows in a Catholic ceremony before a bishop or any delegated priest or deacon, in the presence of two other witnesses. A Catholic may marry without a Catholic clergyman, in the presence of two witnesses, when there is a danger of death, or when it is judged that no clergyman can come within a month. Marriage in a civil ceremony, for Catholics, is no marriage at all.[6]

Finally, with respect to *mixed marriages* between Catholics and non-Catholics, the Church grants permission for such, but she has a concern for the spiritual welfare of those who enter into such marriages and requires the Catholic spouse to promise to baptize and raise the children in the Faith as a condition for permission.

The Fathers

The Shepherd of Hermas, Mandate 4, 1, 4 (inter AD 140-155)

"What then, sir", said I, "shall the husband do, if the wife continue in this disposition? (i.e., adultery)." "Let him dismiss her", he said, "and let the husband remain single. But if he dismiss his wife and marry another, he too commits adultery." "If, then, sir", said I, "after the wife be dismissed, she repent and wish to return to her own husband, is she not to be received?" "Indeed", he said, "if the husband does not receive her, he sins and brings great sin upon himself. It is necessary, in fact, to receive the sinner who repents ..."

Tertullian, *To My Wife* 2, 8, 6 (inter AD 200-206)

"How shall we suffice for the telling of that happiness of that marriage which the Church arranges, which the sacrifice strengthens, on which the blessing sets a seal, which the angels proclaim, and which has the [Heavenly] Father's approval?"

St Hippolytus of Rome, *Refutation of All Heresies* 9, 12 (post AD 222)

"For this reason women who were reputed to be believers began to take drugs to render themselves sterile, and being conceived, since they would not, on account of relatives and excessive wealth, want to have a child by a slave or by any insignificant person. See, then, into what great impiety that lawless one has proceeded, by teaching adultery and murder at the same time."

---

[6] Cf. *Apologetics and Catholic Doctrine*, Archbishop M. Sheehan, The Saint Austin Press, London, rev. ed. 2001, p. 610.

Origen, *Commentaries on Matthew* **14, 16 (post AD 244)**
"Certainly it is God who joins two in one, so that when He marries a woman to a man, there are no longer two. And since it is God who joins them, there is in this joining a grace for those who are joined by God. Paul knew this, and he said that just as holy celibacy was a grace so also was marriage according to the word of God a grace. He says, 'I would that all men were like myself; but each has his own grace from God, one in this way, another in that.'"

St Cyril of Jerusalem, *Catechetical Lectures* **4, 25 (c. AD 350)**
"Let those also be of good cheer who are married and use their marriage properly; who enter marriage lawfully, and not out of wantonness and unbounded license; who recognize periods of continence so that they may give themselves to prayer; who in the assemblies bring clean bodies as well as clean garments into church; who have embarked upon the matrimonial estate for the procreation of children, and not for the sake of indulgence."

St Ambrose of Milan, *Commentary on Luke* **8, 2 (c. AD 389)**
"If every marriage is from God it is not licit to dissolve any marriage. How, then, does the Apostle say: 'If the unbeliever departs, let him depart?' What is remarkable in this saying is that, far from intending Christians to find in it an excuse for divorce, he shows that not every marriage is in fact from God; for Christians, in God's tribunal, cannot be joined to pagans, when the law forbids it."

The Roman Catechism (1566)

Pt. II, Ch. VIII: The faithful, therefore, are to be taught in the first place that marriage was instituted by God. We read in Genesis that *God created them male and female, and blessed them, saying: "Increase and multiply..."*; and also: *"It is not good for man to be alone: let us make him a help like unto himself."* And a little further on: *But for Adam there was not found a helper like himself. Then the Lord God cast a deep sleep upon Adam; and when he was fast asleep, he took one of his ribs, and filled up flesh for it. And the Lord God* *built a rib which he took from Adam into a woman, and brought her to Adam; and Adam said: "This is now bone of my bones, and flesh of my flesh: she shall be called woman, because she was taken out of man: wherefore a man shall leave father and mother, and shall cleave to his wife; and they shall be two in one flesh."* These words, according to the authority of our Lord Himself, as we read in St Matthew, prove the divine institution of Matrimony.

Catechism of the Catholic Church (1992)

No. 1601: The matrimonial covenant, by which a man and a woman establish between themselves a partnership of the whole of life, is by its nature ordered toward the good of the spouses and the procreation and education of offspring; this covenant between baptized persons has been raised by Christ the Lord to the dignity of a sacrament.

No. 1625: The parties to a marriage covenant are a baptized man and woman, free to contract marriage, who freely express their consent; "to be free" means:

- not being under constraint.
- not impeded by any natural or ecclesiastical law.

No. 1626: The Church holds the exchange of consent between the spouses to be the indispensable element that "makes the marriage." If consent is lacking there is no marriage.

Part II

The Ten Commandments

Introduction

"If you would enter into life, keep the commandments" (Mt 19:17).

The Ten Commandments are the laws of God delivered to the people of Israel through Moses on Mount Sinai. Written originally on two tablets of stone, they were solemnly kept in the Ark of the Covenant. It is generally thought that the first table contained the first three commandments, the second the next seven. In order, they are as follows:

(i) I am the Lord your God, who brought you out of the land of Egypt, out of the house of bondage. You shall have no other gods before me. You shall not make for yourself a graven image, or any likeness of anything that is in heaven above, or that is in the earth beneath, or that is in the water under the earth; you shall not bow down to them or serve them.
(ii) You shall not take the name of the Lord your God in vain.
(iii) Remember the Sabbath day, to keep it holy.
(iv) Honor your father and your mother.
(v) You shall not kill.
(vi) You shall not commit adultery.
(vii) You shall not steal.
(viii) You shall not bear false witness against your neighbor.
(ix) You shall not covet your neighbor's wife.
(x) You shall not covet your neighbor's goods.

There exists no numerical division of the Ten Commandments in the books of Moses, giving rise to a difference in opinion as to their numeration. The Catholic system of numeration is based on the Hebrew text, was made by St Augustine of Hippo in his book *"Questions on Exodus"* (Bk 2, Qu. 71) and was adopted by the Council of Trent. This arrangement makes the first commandment relate to the worship of false gods, with the reference to idols as an application of the precept to adore but one God rather than standing as a separate commandment. The precept forbidding the use of the Lord's Name in vain consequently becomes the second commandment, while the final precept against concupiscence is divided into two - unlawful desires of the flesh becoming the ninth and unlawful desires for the possession of goods becoming the tenth commandment. This division of the Decalogue is also followed by most Lutherans.

The other system of division adopted by most Protestant Churches is based on the authority of Origen, whereby the matter of worship is divided into two separate commandments and the ninth and tenth of the Catholic division are combined into a single tenth. According to the *Catholic Encyclopedia* (1911, Vol. IV, p. 153), "It seems, however, as logical to separate at the end as to group at the beginning, for, while one single object is aimed at under worship, two specifically different sins are forbidden under covetousness; if adultery and theft belong to two distinct species of moral wrong, the same must be said of the desire to commit these evils."

The obligation to observe the Ten Commandments rests not on the fact that they were delivered to Moses, but because they are instilled in the hearts of all, and were perfected and confirmed by Our Lord Jesus Christ Himself: "If you would enter into life, keep the commandments" (Mt 19:17); "He who has my commandments and keeps them, he it is who loves me" (Jn 14:21); "For neither circumcision counts for anything nor uncircumcision, but keeping the commandments of God" (1 Cor. 7:19). Furthermore, the Apostle St John expressly states, "... his commandments are not burdensome" (1 Jn 5:3). God is ever ready to assist those who seek to conform to the Decalogue, leaving no reason for discouragement.

Nevertheless, the Roman Catechism found it necessary to rebuke "those who to their own serious injury, have the impious hardihood to assert that the observance of the law, whether easy or difficult, is by no means necessary to salvation."[1] Martin Luther was one such person who on separate occasions declared:

> We must remove the Decalogue out of sight and heart (*De Wette* 4, 188).[2]

---

[1] Part III, Ch. I.
[2] Quoted in Mgr. P.F. O'Hare, *The Facts about Luther*, TAN Books and Publishers Inc., Rockford, Illinois, 1987, p. 311.

Introduction

The scholastics think that the judicial and ceremonial laws of Moses were abolished by the coming of Christ, but not the moral law. They are blind. When Paul declares that we are delivered from the curse of the Law he means the whole Law, particularly the moral law which more than the other laws accuses, curses, and condemns the conscience. The Ten Commandments have no right to condemn that conscience in which Jesus dwells, for Jesus has taken from the Ten Commandments the right and power to curse (*Commentary on Galatians* 4:10-31, 1535).

If Moses should attempt to intimidate you with his stupid Ten Commandments, tell him right out: chase yourself to the Jews (*Lecture at Wittenburg*).[3]

Contrast these statements with Ps. 19, which celebrates the praises of the Divine Law (vv. 7-8):

"The law of the Lord is perfect, reviving the soul; the testimony of the Lord is sure, making wise the simple; the precepts of the Lord are right, rejoicing the heart; the commandment of the Lord is pure, enlightening the eyes."

Great too are the rewards God has in store for those who serve His glory through the Commandments:

"*... in keeping them there is great reward*" (Ps. 19:11).

"*... your reward is great in heaven*" (Mt 5:12).

"*... good measure, pressed down, shaken together, running over*" (Lk 6:38).

God's glory is thus identified with our advantage.

Finally, all the Commandments form part of a greater law – the law of charity. As St Paul says, "love is the fulfilling of the law" (Rom. 13:10). Our Lord Himself summed up the Law in these words: "you shall love the Lord your God with all your heart, and ... your neighbor as yourself" (Mk 12:30-31).

---

[3] *Ibid.*

The Fathers

St Irenaeus of Lyons, *Against Heresies* 4, 15, 1 (c. AD 180)
"The Lord prescribed love toward God and taught justice towards neighbor, so that man would be neither unjust, nor unworthy of God. Thus, through the Decalogue, God prepared man to become his friend to live in harmony with his neighbor ... The words of the Decalogue remain likewise for us Christians. Far from being abolished, they have received amplification and development from the fact of the coming of the Lord in the flesh ... From the beginning, God had implanted in the heart of man the precepts of the natural law. Then he was content to remind him of them. This was the Decalogue."

Origen, *Homilies on Exodus* 8, 1 (post AD 244)
"Since there was a passing from the paradise of freedom to the slavery of this world, in punishment for sin, the first phrase of the Decalogue, the first word of God's commandments, bears on freedom: 'I am the Lord your God, who brought you out of the land of Egypt, out of the house of slavery.'"

St Augustine of Hippo, *Sermon* 33, 2, 2 (inter AD 391-430)
"As charity comprises the two Commandments to which the Lord related the whole Law and the prophets ... so the Ten Commandments were themselves given on two tablets. Three were written on one tablet and seven on the other."

St Augustine of Hippo, *Sermon* 67 (inter AD 391-430)
"How, I ask, is it said to be impossible for man to love – to love, I say, a beneficent Creator, a most loving Father, and also, in the persons of his brethren, to love his own flesh? Yet, he who loves has fulfilled the law."

St Augustine of Hippo, *Tract 122 on John*, 8 (AD 416-417)
"For if we determine on the number that should indicate the law, what else can it be but ten? For we have absolute certainty that the Decalogue of the law, that is, those ten well-known precepts, were first written by the finger of God on two tables of stone (Deut. 9:10) But the law, when it is not aided by grace, makes transgressors, and is only in the letter, on

account of which the apostle specially declared, 'The letter kills, but the spirit gives life' (2 Cor. 3:6). Let the spirit then be added to the letter, lest the letter kill him whom the spirit makes not alive, and let us work out the precepts of the law, not in our own strength, but by the grace of the Savior."

The Roman Catechism (1566)

Pt. III, Ch. I: The pastor should also teach that the Commandments of God are not difficult ... Hence the Apostle St John expressly says that *the commandments of God are not heavy*; for as St Bernard observes, *nothing more just could be exacted from man, nothing that could confer on him a more exalted dignity, nothing more advantageous.* Hence St Augustine, filled with admiration of God's infinite goodness, thus addresses God: *What is man that thou wouldst be loved by him? And if he loves Thee not, Thou threatenest him with heavy punishment. Is it not punishment enough that I love Thee not?*

Catechism of the Catholic Church (1992)

No. 2068: The Council of Trent teaches that the Ten Commandments are obligatory for Christians and that the justified man is still bound to keep them; the Second Vatican Council confirms: "The bishops, successors of the apostles, receive from the Lord ... the mission of teaching all peoples, and of preaching the Gospel to every creature, so that all men may attain salvation through faith, Baptism and the observance of the Commandments."

No. 2069: The Decalogue forms a coherent whole. Each "word" refers to each of the others and to all of them; they reciprocally condition one another. The two tables shed light on one another; they form an organic unity. To transgress one commandment is to infringe all the others. One cannot honor another person without blessing God his Creator. One cannot adore God without loving all men, his creatures. The Decalogue brings man's religious and social life into unity.

The First Commandment

"I am the Lord your God, who brought you out of the land of Egypt, out of the house of bondage. You shall have no other gods before me. You shall not make for yourself a graven image, or any likeness of anything that is in heaven above, or that is in the earth beneath, or that is in the water under the earth; you shall not bow down to them or serve them" (Exod. 20:2-6).

This is the first and principal commandment both in order and in dignity. It requires us to acknowledge God as Lord, to pay him due honor and adoration, while at the same time forbidding us to acknowledge any other god or gods.

The ancient world was rife with the worship of false gods: "For all the gods of the peoples are idols" (Ps. 96:5). The gods of the pagans included demons, stars and planets, the fire or wind, ancestors or even themselves: "Because your heart is proud, and you have said, 'I am a god'" (Ezek. 28:2).

St Thomas Aquinas teaches that reverence is due to every degree of dignity. Being infinite in every perfection, God is entitled to an infinitely higher love and obedience than any creature. We must know Him, believe in Him, hope and love Him, and render that supreme worship (*latria*) which is due to Him alone.

We honor God with interior worship when we make acts of faith, hope and charity and in our mind and hearts perform acts of reverence, adoration and resign humbly to His holy will. We also offer God exterior worship by making such acts as the Sign of the Cross, genuflecting or praying in common.

One sins against the first commandment, therefore, by not having faith, hope and charity in the true God. This includes those who are in heresy by consciously rejecting what Holy Mother Church proposes for belief, those who despair of salvation or trust not in God's goodness, those who rely solely on their own wealth, health or strength of mind or body, and those who fail to attribute every good they possess as having come from God.

The first commandment formally prohibits idolatry, superstition and irreligion:

Idolatry is the sin of giving to any creature, living or not, the adoration or supreme honor due to God alone. Strictly speaking, the word idolatry means "the worship of idols." As shall be seen, it is legitimate to make statues and images for use in religious worship (Exod. 25:18; 2 Chron. 3:7-10), however, one cannot adore or honor them as gods, for "they can neither see, nor hear, nor help us."

Superstition is turning away from God to seek the aid of the Devil, for example, by placing confidence in fortune-tellers, lucky charms, spells, dreams, etc. It is also prohibited to engage in magic, witchcraft, necromancy (summoning up the dead), astrology, omens, as well as vain observance (pointless practices such as lucky charms, etc.). By virtue of our baptismal promises we have renounced Satan and all his pomps and works. Woe to the Christian who dithers between two sides: "If the Lord is God, follow him; but if Baal, then follow him" (1 Kgs 18:21).

Irreligion is non-belief in, or hatred of, God. It includes atheism, agnosticism, impiety, blasphemy, tempting God, profanation and sacrilege of holy persons, places or things, simony and indifferentism. The twentieth century was the first to witness the establishment of regimes that not only professed non-belief in God but also actively persecuted citizens who did. Concerning indifferentism, no Catholic can consent to the proposition that one religion is as good as another, or actively participate in the religious ceremonies or rites of another religion in anything contrary to the Catholic religion. Conversely, within due limits, nobody may be forced to act against his convictions in religious matters, as God requires a free assent to divine truth.

The first commandment not only obliges us to honor and love God, but also to honor and revere everything belonging to Him (*dulia*). This is the reason why the Church venerates and invokes angels and the Blessed who now enjoy the glory of heaven, as well as honoring the bodies and relics of Saints. If the angels rejoice in heaven over the conversion of one sinner (Lk 15:7), will not they and the Saints with them assist those on earth who invoke their aid seeking repentance, the pardon of sins and God's grace? Their love for us impels them to pour out their prayers for those countries and persons over whom they are placed guardians before the throne of God (Tob. 12:12; Rev. 8:3). Jacob invoked the angel with whom he wrestled to bless him before he let him go (Gen. 32:26), as well as another angel whom he saw not: "the angel who has redeemed me from all evil, bless the lads" (Gen. 48:16). And if Scripture itself celebrates the praises of the Saints, why should we now not show them singular honor, as did the sons of the prophets who bowed down to the ground before Elisha at Jericho? (2 Kgs 1:15; also see Sir. 44:4; Heb. 11).

There are not a few, though, who assert that reference to the intercession of the angels and Saints is not necessary as God can hear our prayers without the need for an intercessor and, in any case, there is only one mediator between God and man, namely Jesus Christ (1 Tim. 2:5). Understood properly, Christ is the one *mediator of redemption*, for there is no other name under heaven by which man is saved. Nevertheless, Scripture itself attests that Christ is not the sole *mediator of prayer*. The Holy Spirit "intercedes for us with sighs too deep for words" (Rom. 8:26). There are examples from Scripture itself that show that God occasionally does not answer prayer without a mediator or intercessor. For instance, Abimelech and the friends of Job were only pardoned through the prayers of Abraham (Gen. 20) and of Job. Also, if having Christ as our one mediator precludes the intercession of the Saints, then St Paul should never have recommended himself to the prayers of his brethren on earth, whose prayers would have lessened the importance of Christ's mediatorship no less than the prayers of the Saints in heaven (Rom. 15:30; Heb. 13:18).

Besides honoring the Saints, we also honor their relics and remains. Relics bring to mind the holy lives of the Saints. God, moreover, has often worked miracles through relics, as testified by Scripture:

"... *as soon as the man touched the bones of Elisha, he revived, and stood on his feet* ..." (2 Kgs 13:21).

"... *so that they even carried out the sick into the streets, and laid them on beds and pallets, that as Peter came by at least his shadow might fall on some of them* ..." (Acts 5:15).

"... *so that handkerchiefs or aprons were carried away from his body to the sick, and diseases left them and the evil spirits came out of them*" (Acts 19:12).

On the question of images - whether of painting, engraving or sculpture - we find in Scripture that God Himself commanded such to be made of Cherubim (Exod. 25:18; 1 Kgs 6:23) and the brazen serpent (Num. 21:8). In fact, God expressed His approval of Solomon's Temple after it was completed even though it included numerous images:

"When Solomon had finished building the house of the Lord and the king's house and all that Solomon desired to build, the Lord appeared to Solomon a second time, as he had appeared to him at Gibeon. And the Lord said to him, 'I have heard your prayer and your supplication, which you have made before me; I have consecrated this house which you have built, and put my name there for ever; my eyes and my heart will be there for all time'" (1 Kgs 9:1-3).

Consequently, the only consistent interpretation of the first commandment is that images are only prohibited where they are used to receive adoration as deities, injuring the worship due to God alone, or where they attempt to form a representation of the Deity as if He were *exactly* as depicted. The Jews, in making the image of the golden calf exclaimed, "These are your gods, O Israel, who brought you up out of the land of Egypt", and were denounced as idolaters for they changed "the glory of God for the image of an ox that eats grass" (Exod. 32:4; Ps. 106:20).

However, to represent God by forms under which He appeared in the Scriptures is not contrary to this commandment as these forms only express an attribute or action ascribed to God. Thus, when God is represented as the Ancient of Days seated on a throne, or the Holy Spirit as a dove, or as tongues of fire, the eternity or love of God is represented. No one is so ignorant as to believe that such forms represent the Deity as He actually is.

Images of Christ, His Holy Mother and of the Saints have always been placed in Catholic churches and homes, not only to be honored, but also to bring to our minds the example of their lives and virtues. Honor and respect given to such images are referred to their prototypes. The Catholic doctrine on the veneration of images was fully defined by the Second Council of Nicaea in AD 787:

Proceeding as it were on the royal road and following the divinely inspired teaching of our holy Fathers, and the tradition of the Catholic Church (for we know that this tradition is of the Holy Spirit which dwells in the Church), with all care and exactitude ... images of our Lord and God and Savior Jesus Christ and of our undefiled Lady, the holy Mother of God, and of the honorable angels, and of saintly and holy men ... the beholders be aroused to recollect the originals and to long after them, and to pay the images the tribute of an embrace and a reverence of honor, not to pay to them the actual worship which is according to our faith, and which is proper only to the divine nature: but as to the figure of the venerable and life-giving cross, and to the holy Gospels and the other sacred monuments, so to those images to accord the honor of incense and oblation of lights, as it has been the pious custom of antiquity. For the honor paid to the image passes to its original, and he that adores an image adores in it the person depicted thereby ...

The Fathers

The Martyrdom of St Polycarp 17, 3 (c. AD 155-157)
"Christ we worship as the Son of God, but the martyrs we love as disciples and imitators of the Lord; and rightly so, because of their unsurpassable devotion to their own King and Teacher. With them may we also become companions and fellow disciples. When the centurion saw the contentiousness caused by the Jews, he confiscated the body, and, according to their custom, burned it. Then, at last, we took up his bones, more precious than costly gems and finer than gold, and put them in a suitable place. The Lord will permit us, when we are able, to assemble there in joy and gladness, and to celebrate the birthday of his martyrdom, both in memory of those who have already engaged in the contest, and for the practice and training of those who have yet to fight."

St Justin Martyr, *Dialogue with Trypho the Jew* 11 (c. AD 155)
"There will never be another God, Trypho, and there has been no other since the world began ... than he who made and ordered the universe. We do not think that our God is different from yours. He is the same who brought your fathers out of Egypt 'by his powerful hand and his

outstretched arm.' We do not place our hope in some other god, for there is none, but in the same God as you do: the God of Abraham, Isaac and Jacob."

St Augustine of Hippo, *The City of God* Bk. 1, Ch. 13 (ante AD 413)
"The bodies of the dead, nevertheless, are not to be despised and thrown aside, and least of all, those of the righteous and faithful, which were used in a chaste manner by the Spirit as the organs and vessels for all good works."

St Augustine of Hippo, *The City of God* Bk. 10 (ante AD 417)
"The homage due to man, of which the Apostle spoke when he commanded servants to obey their masters, and which in Greek is called dulia, is distinct from latria, which denotes the homage that consists in the worship of God."

St Augustine of Hippo, *Christian Instruction* II, 20 (ante AD 426)
"Anything invented by man for making and worshipping idols, or for giving Divine worship to a creature or any part of a creature, is superstitious."

St John Damascene, *On Images* 1, 16 (post AD 725)
"Previously God, who has neither a body nor a face, absolutely could not be represented by an image. But now that he has made himself visible in the flesh and has lived with men, I can make an image of that I have seen of God ... and contemplate the glory of the Lord, his face unveiled."

St John Damascene, *The Source of Knowledge* 4, 17 (post AD 743)
"Who can represent God, invisible as He is incorporeal, uncircumscribed by limits, and incapable of being reproduced under any shape?"

The Roman Catechism (1566)

Pt. III, Ch. II: The (mandatory part) contains a precept of faith, hope and charity. For, acknowledging God to be immovable, immutable, always the same, we rightly confess that He is faithful and entirely just.

Hence in assenting to His oracles, we necessarily yield to Him all belief and obedience. Again, who can contemplate His omnipotence, His clemency, His willing beneficence, and not repose in Him all his hopes? Finally, who can behold the riches of His goodness and love, which He lavishes on us, and not love Him? Hence the exordium and the conclusion used by God in Scripture when giving His commands: *I, the Lord.*

Catechism of the Catholic Church (1992)

No. 2112: The First Commandment condemns polytheism. It requires man neither to believe in, nor to venerate, other divinities than the one true God. Scripture constantly recalls this rejection of "idols (of) silver and gold, the work of men's hands. They have mouths, but do not speak; eyes, but do not see." These empty idols make their worshippers empty: "Those who make them are like them; so are all who trust in them." God, however, is the "living God" who gives life and intervenes in history.

No. 2118: God's first commandment condemns the main sins of irreligion: tempting God, in words or deeds, sacrilege and simony.

No. 2132: The Christian veneration of images is not contrary to the first commandment which proscribes idols. Indeed, "the honor rendered to an image passes to its prototype", and "whoever venerates an image venerates the person portrayed in it." The honor paid to sacred images is a "respectful veneration", not the adoration due to God alone:

> Religious worship is not directed to images in themselves but under their distinctive aspect as images leading us on to God incarnate. The movement toward the image does not terminate in it as image, but tends toward that whose image it is (St Thomas Aquinas, S.T., II-II, 81, 3 ad 3).

The Second Commandment

"You shall not take the name of the Lord your God in vain" (Exod. 20:7).

God, who requires that supreme honor must be paid to Him, also requires that His holy Name be spoken of with reverence and love. The second commandment commands us to honor the Name of God, while prohibiting us from taking it in vain, or swearing by it unnecessarily, falsely or rashly.

Scripture refers to God by many names: Yahweh, Adonai, the Lord, Father, the Almighty, Lord of hosts, King of kings, etc. All are entitled to equal honor and veneration. God's name may be honored in various ways. Firstly, when we publicly confess Him as Lord and God, when we proclaim Christ as Savior, when we give religious homage to the word of God, sing His praises under any circumstances, return Him limitless thanks, confidently invoke His aid in prayer.

God's Name may also be taken or used justly in the following circumstances:

(i) To confirm a matter in a lawful oath.
(ii) To sanctify, as in the administering of the sacraments.
(iii) When confessing it publicly.
(iv) In consecrating all our good actions to His greater glory and honor.
(v) When renouncing the Devil and all his works.
(vi) To resist temptation.

The sin most directly against the reverence due to God is blasphemy, which is speaking or thinking contemptuously of God, holy persons or things. To cast insults at God, Our Lady, angels and saints, to ridicule the Mass, the Sacraments, the Scriptures or to attribute to creatures those things which belong to God alone, are all sins of blasphemy. In the Old Testament this was a capital crime: "He who blasphemes the name of the Lord shall be put to death" (Lev. 24:16).

Cursing is also forbidden by this commandment. Cursing dishonors God by involving Him in doing our evil will, to inflict some evil upon another or even ourselves. In addition, to call down evil upon our neighbor goes against Christ's call of charity: "You shall love your neighbor as yourself" (Mk 12:31).

Profanity falls within the second commandment. To quote the Scriptures without respect, to use foul language in conversation is profane, and unbecoming to the lips of a Christian: "Let no evil talk come out of your mouths, but only such as is good for edifying, as fits the occasion, that it may impart grace to those who hear" (Eph. 4:29).

With regard to the taking of oaths, we honor God's name when we call upon Him to witness the truth of what we say, or our sincerity in our promises. For an oath to be lawful it must be made "in truth, in justice, and in uprightness" (Jer. 4:2).

That truth is necessary to an oath is declared by David: "who swears to his own hurt and does not change" (Ps. 15:4). God is not ignorant for before him "all are open and laid bare" (Heb. 4:13); nor does He love a lie but rather "abhors bloodthirsty and deceitful men" (Ps. 5:6). Oaths taken to do what is unjust or unlawful are sinful both in the oath's taking and in its execution. Such was the oath taken by the Jews who bound themselves not to eat until they had killed St Paul (Acts 23:12).

Justice dictates that in everyday life an oath is not necessary, and that we must satisfy ourselves with simply affirming or denying. Unnecessary oaths are disrespectful to God because they are often made without reflection or for trivial reasons. Matters that are in controversy may be confirmed by oaths: "in all their disputes an oath is final for confirmation" (Heb. 6:16). St Thomas Aquinas equates oaths to the taking of medicine "which is never taken continually but only in times of necessity."

However, some claim that since the coming of Christ, the taking of any oath is forbidden altogether: "Again you have heard that it was said to the men of old, 'You shall not swear falsely, but shall perform to the Lord what you have sworn.' But I say to you, Do not swear at all, either by heaven, for it is the throne of God, or by the earth, for it is his footstool, or by Jerusalem, for it is the city of the great King. And do not swear by your head, for you cannot make one hair white or black. Let what you say be simply 'Yes' or 'No'; anything more than this comes from evil" (Mt 5:33-37).

It cannot be said that these words prohibit all oaths under all circumstances for the Apostles and even the angels make use of oaths:

"But I call God to witness against me – it was to spare you that I refrained from coming to Corinth ..." (2 Cor. 1:23).

"And the angel whom I saw standing on sea and land lifted up his right hand to heaven and swore by him who lives for ever and ever, who created heaven and what is in it, the earth and what is in it, and the sea and what is in it, that there should be no more delay" (Rev. 10:5-6).

What Our Lord was condemning was the perverse practice of some Jews of His day, who asserted that the only prerequisite for a lawful oath was to avoid a lie. Hence, they did not hesitate to make widespread use of oaths in matters most trivial and unimportant, and to demand likewise from others.

The second commandment also requires us to keep our vows: "When you make a vow to the Lord your God, you shall not be slack to pay it; for the Lord your God will surely require it of you, and it would be sin in you" (Deut. 23:21). A vow is a deliberate and free promise made to God to do something good under pain of sin. This sin will be grave or light depending on what is vowed and one's intentions.

Vows are pleasing to God because they are voluntary offerings made to Him. We find God on a number of occasions pleased to accept the vows of His servants:

"Then Jacob made a vow, saying, 'If God will be with me, and will keep me in this way that I go, and will give me bread to eat and clothing to wear, so that I come again to my father's house in peace, then the Lord shall be my God ..." (Gen. 28:20-21).

"And she (Anna) vowed a vow and said, 'O Lord of hosts, if thou wilt indeed look on the affliction of thy maidservant, and remember me, and not forget thy maidservant, but wilt give to thy maidservant a son, then I will give him to the

Lord all the days of his life, and no razor shall touch his head" (1 Sam. 1:11).

By virtue of the power that Our Lord Jesus Christ gave to His Church of binding and loosing, She can, where justice requires, dispense a person from a vow, or change the good work vowed for some other good work. This would normally be the case where to do the act vowed is now impossible, unlawful or unadvisable. For a good reason, a priest in Confession could release a person from a private vow.

The Fathers

St Ambrose, *The Duties of the Clergy* 1, 50, 264 (c. AD 391)
"Sometimes it is wrong to fulfill a promise, and to keep an oath; as Herod, who granted the slaying of John, rather than refuse what he had promised."

St John Chrysostom, *Instructions to Catechumens* 5 (post AD 382)
"But in order not to confuse your minds by saying everything at once today, we put before you one custom, namely, about the avoidance of oaths, saying this much by way of preface, and speaking plainly–[he *proceeds to talk about unnecessary oath taking*] ... For this error is grave, and it is exceedingly grave because it does not seem to be grave, and on this account I fear it, because no one fears it. On this account the disease is incurable, because it does not seem to be a disease; but just as simple speech is not a crime, so neither does this seem to be a crime, but with much boldness this transgression is committed: and if any one call it in question, straightway laughter follows, and much ridicule, not of those who are called in question for their oaths, but of those who wish to rectify the disease."

St Augustine of Hippo, *The Lord's Sermon on the Mount in Matthew* 1, 17 (inter AD 392-396)
"If you have to swear, note that the necessity arises from the infirmity of those whom you convince, which infirmity is indeed an evil. Accordingly, He did not say: 'that which is over and above is evil' but 'is of evil.' For you do not evil; since you make good use of swearing, by persuading

another to a useful purpose: yet it 'comes of the evil' of the person by whose infirmity you are forced to swear."

St Augustine of Hippo, *To Armentius and Paulinus* Ep. 127 (AD 411-412)
"Since you have taken a vow, you have bound yourself: you cannot do otherwise. If you do not do what you have vowed, you will not be as you would have been, had you not vowed. For then you would have been less great, not less good: whereas now if you break faith with God (which God forbid) you are the more unhappy, just as you would have been happier, had you kept your vow."

The Roman Catechism (1566)

Pt. III, Ch. III: *For he who requires that honor be paid him, also requires that he be spoken of with reverence, and must forbid the contrary, as is clearly shown by these words of the Lord in Malachy:* "The son honoreth the father, and the servant his master; if then I be a father, where is my honor?"

However, on account of the importance of the obligation, God wished to make the law, which commands His own divine and most holy Name to be honored, a distinct commandment, expressed in the clearest and simplest terms.

Catechism of the Catholic Church (1992)

No. 2153: In the Sermon on the Mount, Jesus explained the second commandment: "You have heard that it was said to the men of old, 'You shall not swear falsely, but shall perform to the Lord what you have sworn.' But I say to you, Do not swear at all ... Let what you say be simply 'Yes' or 'No'; anything more than this comes from the evil one." Jesus teaches that every oath involves a reference to God and that God's presence and his truth must be honored in all speech. Discretion in calling upon God is allied with a respectful awareness of his presence, which all our assertions either witness to or mock.

No. 2155: The holiness of the divine name demands that we neither use it for trivial matters, nor take an oath which on the basis of the circumstances could be interpreted as approval of an authority unjustly requiring it. When an oath is required by illegitimate civil authorities, it may be refused. It must be refused when it is required for purposes contrary to the dignity of persons or to ecclesial communion.

The Third Commandment

"Remember the Sabbath day, to keep it holy" (Exod. 20:8).

If we sincerely and devoutly worship God, we should employ as much of our time in His service, and sanctify all our actions by directing them to His greater glory and honor. However, since we cannot easily discharge these obligations while engaged in the affairs of the world, God has appointed one day of the week for us to give Him public worship and render Him homage.

The law of the Sabbath extends back to creation of man: "... for in six days the Lord made heaven and earth, the sea, and all that is in them, and rested the seventh day; therefore the Lord blessed the sabbath day and hallowed it" (Exod. 20:11). God desired that one day be set aside to remember that He created all things in six days, and then rested from the creation of new creatures on the seventh.

For Christians, the Church during Apostolic times transferred the day of rest from the seventh day to the first of the week – the *Lord's Day* – to show that the Jewish law and ceremonies were now superseded and to honor the day of Our Lord's resurrection from the dead. The concept of the Lord's Day is found in the Book of Revelation:

"John, your brother, who share with you in Jesus the tribulation and the kingdom and the patient endurance, was on the island called Patmos ... I was in the Spirit on the Lord's day..." (1:9-10).

The Jews kept holy the Sabbath in honor of the first creation; Christians recognize that Christ by His resurrection effected a new creation. The other commandments are precepts of the natural law and hence are unalterable. This part of the third commandment belongs to the ceremonial law; nature does not instruct us to worship God publicly on the seventh day rather than any other.

In any case it is clear from Scripture that the observance of the Sabbath was to be abrogated with the coming of Christ: "Therefore let no one pass judgment on you in questions of food and drink or with regard to a festival or a new moon or a *sabbath*. These are only a shadow of what is to come; but the substance belongs to Christ" (Col. 2:16-17). Nevertheless, according to St Thomas Aquinas, Christians "keep the Saturdays in veneration of the Blessed Virgin, in whom remained a firm faith on that Saturday while Christ was dead."

The third commandment requires that we sanctify the Sabbath by rest and worship. Canon 1247 of the *Code of Canon Law* promulgated by Pope St John Paul II in 1983, sets out our obligations here. *Worship:* "On Sundays and other Holydays of Obligation, the faithful are obliged to participate at Mass." *Rest:* "They should also abstain from such work or business as would hinder the worship owed to God, the joy proper to the Lord's Day, or the due relaxation of mind and body."

The obligation to attend Mass is a serious one: "Those who deliberately transgress this obligation commit a grave sin."[1] We are obliged to hear the whole of Mass, and to miss any part without proper cause is wrong, and wilfully to miss a considerable or essential part, sinful. Legitimate reasons dispense a Catholic from this duty, for example, illness, the care of the sick or helpless, unavoidable work, excessive distance from church.

In modern times, more work, sport and business transactions are indiscriminately carried out on Sundays, desacralizing this most holy day and making it more difficult for Christians to fulfill their spiritual obligations. This has often occurred with the support of government legislation. It virtually amounts to a return to the conditions Christians had to endure during the days of the Roman Empire before the rise of Constantine. Hence the following words of Pope St John Paul II:

> Therefore, also in the particular circumstances of our time, Christians will naturally strive to ensure that civil legislation respects their duty to keep Sunday holy. In any case, they are obliged in conscience to arrange their Sunday rest in a way which allows them to take part in the Eucharist, refraining from work and activities which are incompatible with the sanctification of the Lord's Day, with its characteristic joy and necessary rest for spirit and body.[2]

---

[1] CCC #2181.
[2] *Dies Domini* #67, 1998.

To attend Mass devoutly, to listen to the word of God, to read spiritual books, to visit the sick or afflicted, are all works which go to sanctify the Lord's Day.

The observance of Sunday is a public profession of our faith. Public prayers offered in the name of the Church, and by Her priests, are more powerful than our own private devotions.

With the coming of Our Lord Jesus Christ, a more perfect understanding of the Sabbath law was inaugurated: "The sabbath was made for man, not man for the sabbath; so the Son of man is lord even of the sabbath" (Mk 2:27-28). All work that relates to our daily necessities and cares of the household is allowed as long as they do not expose us to the danger of missing Mass.

While it is better to avoid our normal weekday employment on the Lord's Day, work can be done on a Sunday for good reasons:

(i) *Necessity*: when one's work roster, or necessary income, obliges one to work.
(ii) *Emergency*: fire, flood, bad weather: "What man of you, if he has one sheep and it falls into a pit on the sabbath, will not lay hold of it and lift it out?" (Mt 12:11).
(iii) *Piety*: work done in the service of God, for example, adorning a church: "the priests in the temple profane the sabbath, and are guiltless" (Mt 12:5).
(iv) *Our neighbor's good*: to help the sick or poor: "Religion that is pure and undefiled before God and the Father is this: to visit orphans and widows in their affliction ..." (Js. 1:27).

The Jewish leaders did not make allowance for everyday human needs and were overly legalistic in their observance of the Sabbath. Our Lord openly defied their legalism while remaining true to the Law of Moses:

(i) The woman in the Synagogue (Lk 12:10-17).
(ii) The plucking of ears of corn by the Disciples (Mk 2:23).
(iii) The withered hand (Mk 3:1-6).
(iv) The infirm man at the poolside (Jn 5:2-18).
(v) The man born blind (Jn 9:1-41).

From the very beginning of the Church, other days have been set aside to celebrate the mysteries of our redemption, the glories of the Blessed Virgin Mary, the Apostles, Martyrs, Virgins and other Saints who now reign with Christ. Holy Days of Obligation vary from country to country and from time to time and may impose obligations of observance identical to Sundays. Due to conditions of modern secular society, however, the faithful are today usually only called upon to hear Mass on such feast days.

The Fathers

St Ignatius of Antioch, *Letter to the Magnesians* 9, 1 (c. AD 110)
"Those who walked in ancient customs came to a new hope, no longer following the Sabbath but living by the Lord's Day, on which we came to life through Him and through His death."

Letter to Diognetus 4, 1 (inter AD 125-200)
"Furthermore, I do not suppose that you need to learn from me how ridiculous and unworthy of any argument are their scruples about food, their superstition about the Sabbath, their pride in circumcision and their sham in fasting."

St Justin Martyr, *Dialogue with Trypho the Jew* 23 (c. AD 155)
"If circumcision was not necessary before Abraham, nor before Moses the Sabbath observance and festivals and sacrifices, then, similarly they are not necessary now, when in accordance with the will of God, Jesus Christ the Son of God has been born without sin, of a Virgin of the offspring of Abraham."

St Augustine of Hippo, *Against Faustus the Manichean* 18, 4 (AD 400)
"The things in the Law and in the Prophets which Christians do not observe are those which only signified the things they do observe. They were but figures of things to come, which figures, now that the things themselves have been revealed and made present by Christ, must be removed, so that in the very fact of their removal the Law and the Prophets may be fulfilled."

St Leo I, *Sermons* 63, 5 (ante AD 461)
"For all things that, according to the Law, were prior, whether circumcision of the flesh, or the multitude of sacrificial victims, or the observance of the Sabbath, testified to Christ and foretold Christ's grace. And He is the end of the Law, not by annulling but by fulfilling what is signified."

The Roman Catechism (1566)

Pt. II, Ch. IV: This Commandment of the Law rightly and in due order prescribes the external worship which we owe to God; for it is, as it were, a consequence of the preceding Commandment. For if we sincerely and devoutly worship God, guided by the faith and hope we have in Him, we cannot but honor Him with external worship and thanksgiving. Now since we cannot easily discharge these duties while occupied in worldly affairs, a certain fixed time has been set aside so that it may be conveniently performed.

Catechism of the Catholic Church (1992)

No. 2176: The celebration of Sunday observes the moral commandment inscribed by nature in the human heart to render to God an outward, visible, public, and regular worship "as a sign of his universal beneficence to all." Sunday worship fulfills the moral command of the Old Covenant, taking up its rhythm and spirit in the weekly celebration of the Creator and Redeemer of his people.

No. 2185: On Sundays and other holy days of obligation, the faithful are to refrain from engaging in work or activities that hinder the worship owed to God, the joy proper to the Lord's Day, the performance of the works of mercy, and the appropriate relaxation of mind and body. Family needs or important social service can legitimately excuse from the obligation of Sunday rest. The faithful should see to it that legitimate excuses do not lead to habits prejudicial to religion, family life, and health.

The Fourth Commandment

"Honor your father and your mother" (Exod. 20:12).

The first three commandments relate directly to God; the next seven, our neighbor. We are obliged to love our neighbor on account of God, hence Our Lord's declarations that "you shall love the Lord your God with all your heart ..." and "You shall love your neighbor as yourself" (Mk 12:29-31). Also, "he who does not love his brother whom he has seen, cannot love God whom he has not seen" (1 Jn 4:20).

As Christians we are bound to love all but we are not bound to do good to all. Hence, the fourth commandment is concerned with the duties owed by children to their parents and, by implication, parents to their children. Among all classes of relatives there are none closer than our parents. Besides our parents, there are others whose positions of authority or superiority entitle them to parental honor.

Nothing is more excellent in the life of Christians than ready obedience. The Evangelists in the four Gospels relate nothing of Our Lord's life from His twelfth to thirtieth year except that He lived under the authority of the Blessed Virgin Mary and St Joseph: "And he went down with them and came to Nazareth, and was obedient to them" (Lk 2:51).

By the fourth commandment we are obliged to "honor" our parents. Honor includes love, respect, obedience and reverence. It combines both fear and love. To honor is therefore to give the highest esteem that can be given to anyone. In honoring our parents we honor ourselves "(f)or a man's glory comes from honoring his father, and it is a disgrace for children not to respect their mother" (Sir. 3:11).

Besides our natural father, there are others called fathers in Scripture to whom honor is due. Prelates of the Church are called fathers: "I do not write this to make you ashamed, but to admonish you as my beloved children. For though you have countless guides in Christ, you do not have many fathers. For I became your father in Christ Jesus through the gospel" (1 Cor. 4:14-15). We call priests "father" because they have spiritual care over all the people of God. Consequently, they are entitled to receive honor and whatever is necessary for their support: "Fear the

Lord and honor the priest, and give him his portion, as is commanded you: the first fruits, the guilt offering, the gift of the shoulders, the sacrifice of sanctification, and the first fruits of the holy things" (Sir. 7:31); "Obey your leaders and submit to them; for they are keeping watch over your souls, as men who will have to give account" (Heb. 13:17); "Let the elders who rule well be considered worthy of double honor, especially those who labor in preaching and teaching" (1 Tim. 5:17).

Father, as a name, is also given to those in positions of care, fidelity and wisdom such as teachers, guardians and the aged (2 Kgs 2:12; 13:14), as well as to those who are entrusted with government, power or command (2 Kgs 5:13). St Peter states: "Now who is there to harm you if you are zealous for what is right? But even if you do suffer for righteousness' sake, you will be blessed. Have no fear of them, nor be troubled" (1 Pet. 2:13-14); likewise, St Paul: "Let every person be subject to the governing authorities. For there is no authority except from God" (Rom. 13:1). However, where their commands are unjust or perverse, they must not be obeyed, since they no longer rule according to rightful authority: "We must obey God rather than men" (Acts 5:29).

In all fatherly figures we behold figures of the immortal God and images of the divine power, and through them we give homage to the providence of God who has entrusted to them the care of family, Church and public affairs as His instruments. Of all fatherly figures it can therefore be said "He who hears you hears me, and he who rejects you rejects me" (Lk 10:16).

Though occupying a somewhat different position, mothers are no less deserving of honor under this commandment. It must never be far from our minds what benefits and care they give us, and the enormous labor and effort with which they brought us up. When approached by his mother, Solomon rose up to meet her, and after paying her due respect, placed her on a throne to his right hand (1 Kgs 2:19).

Scripture speaks repeatedly on the honor children should give to parents:

"Whoever honors his father will be gladdened by his own children, and when he prays he will be heard. Whoever glorifies his father will have long life, and whoever obeys the Lord will refresh his mother" (Sir. 3:5-6).

"O son, help your father in his old age, and do not grieve him as long as he lives; even if he is lacking in understanding, show forbearance; in all your strength do not despise him. For kindness to a father will not be forgotten, and against your sins it will be credited to you" (Sir. 3:12-14).

"Children, obey your parents in everything, for this pleases the Lord" (Col. 3:20).

From all this it follows that it is forbidden to do anything that may tend to damage the honor which we owe to our parents: harboring feelings of dislike or hatred, using injurious language towards them, to wish them evil, to give them unnecessary trouble or anxiety, to anger them, to neglect to pray for them, to threaten them, to raise our hand against them, to refuse to obey them or listen to their advice. The duty of obedience is modified when the children are of age, but children are never free from the obligation of love and reverence.

The fourth commandment conversely requires parents to properly fulfil the many duties they themselves owe to their children. The great thought of parents should be to bring up their children for God, as they hold the place of God in their families. Parents must do all things necessary to preserve their children in life and health, and have them baptized within one month after birth (cf. canon 867). Parents must also instruct and correct them, set them a good example, and have them properly instructed in the Faith: "Fathers, do not provoke your children to anger, but bring them up in the discipline and instruction of the Lord" (Eph. 6:4); "The rod and reproof give wisdom, but a child left to himself brings shame to his mother" (Prov. 29:15).

Children, however, are to prefer the will of God and His law to the desires of their parents: "If any one comes to me and does not hate his own father and mother and wife and children and brothers and sisters, yes, and even his own life, he cannot be my disciple" (Lk 14:26). Parents must also never unduly oppose a religious vocation in their children: "He who loves father or mother more than me is not worthy of me" (Mt 10:37).

In the Old Testament, the reward promised for the observance of this commandment was great and consisted in long life: "that your days may be prolonged, and that it may go well with you" (Deut. 5:16). But the punishments for those who failed to honor were equally great: "everyone who curses his father or his mother shall be put to death" (Lev. 20:9); "He who does violence to his father and chases away his mother is a son who causes shame and brings reproach" (Prov. 19:26). As St Thomas Aquinas says, "if you do not acknowledge the blessing of the natural life which you owe to your parents, then you are unworthy of the life of grace, which is greater, and all the more so for the life of glory, which is the greatest of all blessings."

The Fathers

Letter to Diognetus 5, 1 (inter AD 125-200)
"(Christians) reside in their own nations, but as resident aliens. They participate in all things as citizens and endure all things as foreigners ... They obey the established laws and their way of life surpasses the laws ... So noble is the position to which God has assigned them that they are not allowed to desert it."

Origen, *Homilies on the Canticle of Canticles* Hom. 2 (c. AD 240-242)
"We ought to love God first, then our parents, then our children, and lastly those of our household."

St John Chrysostom, *Homilies on First Corinthians* Hom. 26 (c. AD 392)
"... when we exhort children to be obedient to parents, saying, that it is written, honor thy father and thy mother, they reply to us, 'mention also what follows, and you fathers, provoke not your children to wrath' (Eph. 6:4). And servants when we tell them that it is written that they should obey their masters, and not serve with eye-service, they also again demand of us what follows, bidding us also give the same advice to masters."

St Augustine of Hippo, *Christian Instruction* 1, 28 (AD 397 et 426)
"One ought to love all men equally. Since, however, one cannot do good to all, we ought to consider those chiefly who by reason of place, time or any other circumstance, by a kind of chance, are more closely united to us."

St Gregory the Great, *Moral Teachings from the Book of Job* Bk. 35 (AD 595)
"Obedience should be practised, not out of servile fear, but from a sense of charity, not through fear of punishment, but through love of justice."

The Roman Catechism (1566)

Pt. III, Ch. V: (Parents) are, so to say, images of the immortal God. In them we behold a picture of our own origin; from them we have received existence, them God made use of to infuse into us a soul and reason, by them we were led to the Sacraments, instructed in our religion, schooled in right conduct and holiness, and trained in civil and human knowledge.

Catechism of the Catholic Church (1992)

No. 2217: As long as a child lives at home with his parents, the child should obey his parents in all that they ask of him when it is for his good or that of the family. "Children, obey your parents in everything, for this pleases the Lord." Children should also obey the reasonable directions of their teachers and all to whom their parents have entrusted them. But if a child is convinced in conscience that it would be morally wrong to obey a particular order, he must not do so.

No. 2232: Family ties are important but not absolute. Just as the child grows to maturity and human and spiritual autonomy, so his unique vocation which comes from God asserts itself more clearly and forcefully. Parents should respect this call and encourage their children to follow it. They must be convinced that the first vocation of the Christian is to follow Jesus: "He who loves father or mother more than me is not worthy of me; and he who loves son or daughter more than me is not worthy of me."

The Fifth Commandment

"You shall not kill" (Exod. 20:13).

The fifth commandment imposes a two-fold obligation: the first is prohibitory and forbids all wilful murder, the unjust taking of another's life, all thoughts, words or deeds tending to this, the taking of one's own life, all other things that may shorten or endanger it without necessity, and the 'murder' of our neighbor's soul by bad example, or scandal; the other is mandatory and requires us to promote sentiments of charity and peace with all others, to have concord and friendship with our enemies, and to endure every inconvenience with patience.

Murder is one of the four sins that *"cry out to heaven for vengeance"* and is the unlawful putting to death of a person with premeditated malice or grave negligence. This commandment recognizes no exception, all are forbidden to kill. Conversely, no individual, of whatever station in life, is without protection under this law. Furthermore, not only is the act of murder prohibited, but also any counsel, assistance, help or guidance given to bring about its accomplishment. The guilt of murder is also attached when death is caused by carelessness, recklessness or want of proper precaution. Murder includes abortion.

Suicide, or self-murder, also falls within the words "you shall not kill." To suicide is to usurp God's rights since He, not we, is the master of our lives. Nor can we expose our life or health to danger unless a higher duty requires it, or to obtain a greater good. Suicide includes euthanasia.

Unjust anger, hatred, revenge, fighting and quarrelling all can lead to unlawful killing and therefore are prohibited. As St Thomas Aquinas says, "the Lord wishes us to avoid the beginnings of sins; and anger is thus to be avoided for it is the beginning of murder." Anger can be holy but it must be within just bounds, moderate and have a just cause for it: "Let every man be quick to hear, slow to speak, slow to anger" (Js. 1:19). Hatred wishes evil and is the opposite of fraternal charity: "But I say to you that every one who is angry with his brother shall be liable to judgment" (Mt 5:22); "Any one who hates his brother is a murderer" (1 Jn 3:15).

Revenge is the giving of evil for evil, the deliberate infliction of injury in return for an injury received. Fighting, quarrelling and injurious words can sometimes tend to murder and are works of the flesh: "I warn you, as I warned you before, that those who do such things shall not inherit the kingdom of God" (Gal. 5:19-21).

Scandal is the doing of evil with the intention of inciting another to sin, for example, when one causes another to commit adultery, theft, lie, etc. Scandal is indirect when, without meaning to cause another to sin, but foreseeing that they may do so, a person does or says before others something wrong and of a nature to cause them to sin.

Scandal is a real evil condemned by Our Lord: "but whoever causes one of these little ones who believe in me to sin, it would be better for him to have a great millstone fastened round his neck and to be drowned in the depth of the sea. Woe to the world for temptations to sin!" (Mt 18:6-7).

It is permitted to kill animals for proper nourishment. It is in accord with nature that plants nourish animals, certain animals nourish others and that both plants and animals nourish man: "Every moving thing that lives shall be food for you; and as I gave you the green plants, I give you everything" (Gen. 9:3).

The killing of another is not always sinful. Unintentional accidental death, caused without negligence, involves no guilt: "If any one kills his neighbor unintentionally without having been at enmity with him in time past ... he may flee to one of these cities and save his life" (Deut. 19:4-5).

Civil authorities may inflict punishments by legal exercise in legitimate revenge for crime to protect the innocent and repress outrage: "Morning by morning I will destroy all the wicked in the land, cutting off all the evildoers from the city of the Lord" (Ps. 101:8); "But if you do wrong, be afraid, for he does not bear the sword in vain; he is the servant of God to execute his wrath on the wrongdoer" (Rom. 13:4). That which is lawful to God is also lawful for His legitimate representatives acting in accord with their mandate.

Likewise, soldiers killing in a just war against an unjust aggressor do not sin. After killing thousands in a single day, the sons of Levi were addressed by Moses as follows: "Today you have ordained yourselves for the service of the Lord" (Exod. 32:29). Such is also the case with one who kills another in proportionate self-defense.

The mandatory part of the fifth commandment inculcates the duty of charity towards all without exception. Charity has a number of facets: "Love is patient and kind; love is not jealous or boastful; it is not arrogant or rude. Love does not insist on its own way; it is not irritable or resentful; it does not rejoice at wrong, but rejoices in the right. Love bears all things, believes all things, hopes all things, endures all things. Love never ends; as for prophecies, they will pass away; as for tongues, they will cease; as for knowledge, it will pass away" (1 Cor. 13:4-8). Charity extends to our enemies: "But I say to you, Love your enemies and pray for those who persecute you" (Mt 5:44); "if your enemy is hungry, feed him; if he is thirsty, give him drink; for by so doing you will heap burning coals upon his head" (Rom. 12:20).

The fullest expression of charity is to pardon and forgive those who have caused us injuries: "So if you are offering your gift at the altar, and there remember that your brother has something against you, leave your gift there before the altar and go; first be reconciled to your brother, and then come and offer your gift" (Mt 5:23-24). So important is this counsel that God refuses pardon to those who do not follow it. Forgiveness of our enemies perfects our nature, for by it we are made like to God who "makes his sun rise on the evil and on the good, and sends rain on the just and on the unjust" (Mt 5:45); "Father, forgive them; for they know not what they do" (Lk 23:34).

The Fathers

St John Chrysostom, *Homilies on Matthew* Hom. 11 (c. AD 390)
"He that is angry without cause, shall be in danger; but he that is angry with cause, shall not be in danger; for without anger, teaching will be useless, judgments unstable, crimes unchecked ... He who is not angry, whereas he has cause to be, sins. For unreasonable patience is the hotbed of many vices, it fosters negligence, and incites not only the wicked but even the good to do wrong."

St Augustine of Hippo, *To Publicola* **Ep. 47 (AD 398)**
"When we do a thing for a good and lawful purpose, if thereby we unintentionally cause harm to anyone, it should by no means be imputed to us."

St Augustine of Hippo, *The City of God* **Bk. 1, Ch. 27 (AD 413)**
"A man who, without exercising public authority, kills an evildoer, shall be judged guilty of murder, and all the more, since he has dared to usurp a power which God has not given him ... The words 'thou shalt not kill' refer to the killing of a man; therefore, not even yourself. For he who kills himself, kills nothing else than a man."

St Augustine of Hippo, *The City of God* **Bk. 19, Ch. 15 (ante AD 427)**
"For even when we wage a just war, our adversaries must be sinning, and every victory, even though gained by wicked men, is a result of the first judgment of God, who humbles the vanquished either for the sake of removing or punishing their sins."

St Gregory the Great, *Moral Teachings from Job* **Bk. 22, 11 (AD 595)**
"It very often happens that without charity being lost, both the destruction of an enemy gladdens us, and his glory, without any sin of envy, saddens us, since, when he falls, we believe that some are deservedly set up, and when he prospers, we dread lest many suffer unjustly."

The Roman Catechism (1566)

Pt. II, Ch. VI: The Christian, instructed in the interpretation of Christ, has learned that the precept is spiritual, and that it commands us not only to keep our hands unstained, but our hearts pure and undefiled; hence what the Jews regarded as quite sufficient, is not sufficient at all. For the Gospel has taught that it is unlawful even to be angry with anyone: *But I say to you that whosoever is angry with his brother, shall be in danger of the judgment. And whosoever shall say to his brother, "Raca", shall be in danger of the council. And whosoever shall say, "Thou fool", shall be in danger of hell fire.*

Catechism of the Catholic Church (1992)

No. 2268: The Fifth Commandment forbids direct and intentional killing as gravely sinful. The murderer and those who co-operate voluntarily in murder commit a sin that cries out to heaven for vengeance.

> Infanticide, fratricide, parricide, and the murder of a spouse are especially grave crimes by reason of the natural bonds which they break. Concern for eugenics or public health cannot justify any murder, even if commanded by public authority.

No. 2322: From its conception, the child has the right to life. Direct abortion, that is, abortion willed as an end or as a means, is a "criminal" practice, gravely contrary to the moral law ... The Church imposes the canonical penalty of excommunication for this crime against human life.

No. 2324: Intentional euthanasia, whatever its forms or motives, is murder. It is gravely contrary to the dignity of the human person and to the respect due to the living God, his Creator.

No. 2325: Suicide is seriously contrary to justice, hope, and charity. It is forbidden by the fifth commandment.

No. 2326: Scandal is a grave offense when by deed or omission it deliberately leads others to sin.

The Sixth Commandment

"You shall not commit adultery" (Exod. 20:14).

The sixth commandment forbids adultery or any sin of impurity with another person's husband or wife while, by implication, inculcating purity of mind and body.

That adultery is the only sin specifically named in this commandment is due to its gravity. One who commits adultery is guilty of a multitude of sins, as is stated in the following verse: "So it is with a woman who leaves her husband ... For first of all, she has disobeyed the law of the Most High; second, she has committed an offense against her husband; and third, she has committed adultery through harlotry and brought forth children by another man" (Sir. 23:22-23).

The bond of wedlock is so strong that neither husband nor wife has power over their own bodies, both being bound by a mutual bond of subjection: "For the wife does not rule over her own body, but the husband does; likewise the husband does not rule over his own body, but the wife does" (1 Cor. 7:4). Consequently, all actions or words that would lead to marital infidelity are equally prohibited for husband and wife.

According to the Law of Moses, the adulterer was stoned to death (Lev. 20:10). Those guilty of adultery were branded with a severe stigma: "He who commits adultery has no sense; he who does it destroys himself. Wounds and dishonor will he get, and his disgrace will not be wiped away" (Prov. 6:32-33). Even where an adulterer may have escaped death, he is plagued with blindness of mind, heart and understanding. No sooner had David fallen into adultery than he became cruel and murderous. Solomon, consumed with lust for pagan women, abandoned the true God to worship idols.

With the coming of Christ, the commandment is raised in understanding to a higher, more spiritual level: "You have heard that it was said, 'You shall not commit adultery.' But I say to you that every one who looks at a woman lustfully has already committed adultery with her in his heart" (Mt 5:27-28).

That all sins of impurity are caught in the prohibition against adultery is clear from both the Old and New Law: "There shall be no cult prostitute of the daughters of Israel" (Deut. 23:17); "Beware, my son, of all immorality" (Tob. 4:12); "For this is the will of God, your sanctification: that you abstain from unchastity" (1 Thes. 4:3); "Do not be deceived; neither the immoral, nor idolaters, nor adulterers, nor homosexuals ... will inherit the kingdom of God" (1 Cor. 6:9-10). By abstaining from other sins of impurity we more easily avoid adultery.

With respect to fornicators, they are said to sin against their own bodies: "Shun immorality. Every other sin which a man commits is outside the body; but the immoral man sins against his own body" (1 Cor. 6:18); "For this is the will of God, your sanctification: that you abstain from unchastity; that each one of you know how to take a wife for himself in holiness and honor, not in the passion of lust like heathen who do not know God" (1 Thes. 4:3-5). Moreover, baptized Christians are "temple(s) of the Holy Spirit" (1 Cor. 6:19) and to defile this temple is to expel the Holy Spirit and to sin against Christ: "Do you not know that your bodies are members of Christ?" (1 Cor. 6:15). Greater, then, is our obligation to cleanse ourselves "from every defilement of body and spirit, and make holiness perfect in the fear of God" (2 Cor. 7:1). Pornography is especially sinful, degrading to man and woman, and offensive to God.

We have to struggle against our evil thoughts and desires all the days of our life: "Has not man a hard service upon earth" (Job 7:1). There are a number of remedies against temptation that consist of action. One should avoid bad company and conversation ("Bad company ruins good morals"[1 Cor. 15:33]), and unrestricted contact with persons of the opposite sex, indecent films, plays, dances, songs, books and magazines: "And if your eye causes you to sin, pluck it out and throw it away" (Mt 18:9).

To keep our bodies in subjection we must pray fervently: "Watch and pray that you may not enter into temptation" (Mt 26:41). Faithful Catholics should frequent the Sacraments very often, especially Holy Communion and Penance and, like St Paul, constantly practise mortification and self-denial: "I pommel my body and subdue it" (1 Cor. 9:27); "for if you live according to the flesh you will die, but if by the Spirit you put to death the deeds of the body you will live" (Rom. 8:13). To those who humble themselves and place their confidence in God a promise is made: "God is faithful, and he will not let you be tempted beyond your strength" (1 Cor. 10:13).

Purity is one of the greatest virtues and brings marvelous peace to the soul. It makes us akin to the angels, enables the Christian to live a life prefiguring the life of glory that awaits us in heaven and is most pleasing in the sight of God.

The Fathers

St Justin Martyr, *First Apology* 15 (c. AD 155)
"According to our Teacher, just as they are sinners who contract a second marriage, even though it be in accord with human law, so also are they sinners who look with lustful desire at a woman. He repudiates not only one who actually commits adultery, but even one who wishes to do so; for not only our actions are manifest to God, but even our thoughts."

Minucius Felix, *The Octavius* 31, 5 (inter AD 218-235)
"We maintain modesty not on the surface but in the mind. We cling freely to the bond of one marriage. In the desire to procreate we know one wife or none. The banquets we attend are not only modest but sober: for we do not indulge in revelry or prolong a feast with strong wine. Rather, we temper our joyousness with gravity. With chaste discourse and even more chaste in body, many of us enjoy rather than boast of the perpetual virginity of a body undefiled. In fact, so far from us is the desire for incest, that some blush even at the thought of a chaste union."

St Cyril of Jerusalem, *Catechetical Lectures* 4, 26 (AD 350)
"And those who are once married – let them not hold in contempt those who have accommodated themselves to a second marriage. Continence is a good and wonderful thing; but still, it is permissible to enter upon a second marriage, lest the weak might fall into fornication."

St Ambrose of Milan, *The Widows* 4, 23 (AD 377-378)
"There are three forms of the virtue of chastity: the first is that of spouses, the second that of widows and the third that of virgins. We do not praise any one of them to the exclusion of the others ... This is the richness of the discipline of the Church ..."

The Roman Catechism (1566)

Pt. III, Ch. VII: The faithful are to be taught and earnestly exhorted to cultivate continence and chastity with all care, to cleanse themselves *from all defilement of the flesh and of the spirit, perfecting sanctification in the fear of God.*

First of all they should be taught that although the virtue of chastity shines with a brighter luster in those who make the holy and religious vow of virginity, nevertheless it is a virtue which belongs also to those who lead a life of celibacy; or who, in the married state, preserve themselves pure and undefiled from unlawful desire.

Catechism of the Catholic Church (1992)

No. 2348: All the baptized are called to chastity. The Christian has "put on Christ", the model for all chastity. All Christ's faithful are called to lead a chaste life in keeping with their particular states of life. At the moment of his Baptism, the Christian is pledged to lead his affective life in chastity.

No. 2381: Adultery is an injustice. He who commits adultery fails in his commitment. He does injury to the sign of the covenant which the marriage bond is, transgresses the rights of the other spouse and undermines the institution of marriage by breaking the contract on which it is based. He compromises the good of human generation and the welfare of children who need their parents' stable union.

No. 2396: Among the sins gravely contrary to chastity are masturbation, fornication, pornography and homosexual practices.

The Seventh Commandment

"You shall not steal" (Exod. 20:15).

Like the preceding commandments, the seventh commandment has two parts. The first prohibits us to injure our neighbor by stealing, robbery, cheating, usury, wilful damage or any other unjust act; the second, by implication, enjoins kindliness and liberality towards our neighbor.

Stealing is the unjust taking away or withholding of goods belonging to another against his will, openly or in secret, when he has a right to possess them. Robbery deprives one of his property through brute force and power. Larceny, or embezzlement, is the secret taking of what belongs to another without the other realizing it. Dishonesty is committed in a multitude of ways, for instance, doing shoddy work, selling defective goods, absenteeism from work without good reason, using an office's resources excessively for personal business. Fraud includes all kinds of cheating in buying and selling: "You shall do no wrong in judgment, in measures of length or weight or quantity" (Lev. 19:35).

It is also a breach of the seventh commandment to assist in stealing: knowingly to buy or receive stolen property; not to return things found or borrowed; to neglect or to refuse to pay our debts. If the true owner cannot be located, the goods should be given to some worthy person or institution in need. They also are guilty who obtain money under false pretenses or deceit, retain to themselves or do not pay customs, taxes or charges of civil authorities, or defraud a laborer of their just wages: "Behold, the wages of the laborers who mowed your fields, which you kept back by fraud, cry out; and the cries of the harvesters have reached the ears of the Lord of hosts!" (Js. 5:4). Corrupt judges bought over by money or other bribes also sin against this commandment: "Your princes are rebels and companions of thieves. Every one loves a bribe and runs after gifts" (Is. 1:23).

To the class of robbers also belong usurers. Usury is the exaction of excessive interest on loans of money above the general practice. Furthermore, the rigorous exaction of what was lent to those who cannot repay is termed rapacity and likewise is a species of robbery.

St Thomas Aquinas includes as thieves those who buy temporal positions of honor or commit the sin of simony: "he who does not enter the sheepfold by the door but climbs in by another way, that man is a thief and a robber" (Jn 10:1). Furthermore, all who take by force lands, provinces or even nations are thieves and are liable to restitution: "Because you have plundered many nations, all the remnant of the peoples shall plunder you" (Hab. 2:8).

The guilt attached to stealing depends on the value of what is stolen. The taking of a small sum as a rule would not be a mortal sin, unless taken from a poor person or if there was an intention of repeating the thefts in order to reach a considerable sum. Nevertheless, we should heed the words of St Paul: "nor thieves, nor the greedy, nor drunkards, nor revilers, nor robbers will inherit the kingdom of God" (1 Cor. 6:10).

When the sin of stealing has been committed it is not enough to simply repent in order to obtain pardon; restitution is necessary. One must give back what has been taken away, or its value, and repair the damage done. Pardon from God cannot be hoped for without restitution. If this cannot be done at once, we must sincerely have the intention of doing so when it is in our power. Restitution is binding not only on the person who commits theft, but also on all who co-operate in the sin: "If you see a thief, you are a friend of his" (Ps. 50:18). The obligation of restitution can only be cancelled by the agreement of the person wronged.

The positive obligation of the seventh commandment enjoins us to relieve the difficulties and distresses of the poor and needy, particularly through the charity of almsgiving. Scripture speaks in numerous passages of this important duty: "It is well with the man who deals generously and lends, who conducts his affairs with justice" (Ps. 112:5); "... lend, expecting nothing in return" (Lk 6:35); "give, and it will be given to you" (Lk 6:38). God will praise and reward those who exercise mercy to the poor, while on the contrary, condemn those who have omitted to do so: "Come, O blessed by my Father, inherit the kingdom prepared for you..."; "Depart from me, you cursed, into the eternal fire" (Mt 25:34-41).

Conversely, those who rely on the charity of others should practise frugality lest they become a burden to them. St Paul was particularly conspicuous in this regard, writing to the Thessalonians: "For you remember our labor and toil, brethren; we worked night and day, that we might not burden any of you, while we preached to you the gospel of God" (1 Thes. 2:9); and elsewhere: "with toil and labor we worked night and day, that we might not burden any of you" (2 Thes. 3:8).

The Fathers

St Basil the Great, *Homily on Luke* **12, 18 (ante AD 379)**
"If you acknowledge them (your temporal goods) as coming from God, is He unjust because He apportions them unequally? Why are you rich while another is poor unless it be that you may have the merit of a good stewardship, and he the reward of patience? It is the hungry man's bread that you withhold, the naked man's cloak that you have stored away, the shoe of the barefoot that you have left to rot, the money of the needy that you have buried underground: and so you injure as many as you might help."

St John Chrysostom, *Homilies on Lazarus* **2, 5 (AD 388)**
"Not to enable the poor to share in our goods is to steal from them and deprive them of life. The goods we possess are not ours, but theirs."

St Ambrose of Milan, *On the Duties of the Clergy* **3, 9, 65 (c. AD 391)**
"Every kind of unfair action is shameful. Even in common things, false weights and unjust measures are accursed. And if fraud in the market or in business is punished, can it seem free from reproach if found in the midst of the performance of the duties of virtue? Solomon says: 'A great and a little weight and divers measures are an abomination before the Lord.' Before that it also says: 'A false balance is abomination to the Lord, but a just weight is acceptable to Him'."

St Augustine of Hippo, *To Macedonius* **Ep. 153 (c. AD 413)**
"Unless a man restore what he has purloined, his sin is not forgiven."

St Gregory the Great, *Book of Pastoral Regulations* **3, 21 (c. AD 591)**
"When we attend to the needs of those in want, we give them what is theirs, not ours. More than performing works of mercy, we are paying a debt of justice."

St Gregory the Great, *Homilies on Ezekiel* 9 (AD 593)
"Let him that has understanding beware lest he withhold his knowledge; let him that has abundance of wealth, watch lest he slacken his merciful bounty; let him who is a servant to art be most solicitous to share his skill and profit with his neighbor. Let him who has an opportunity of speaking with the wealthy man, fear lest he be condemned for burying his talent, if, when he has the chance, he does not plead with him the cause of the poor."

The Roman Catechism (1566)

Pt. III, Ch. VIII: To inspire the faithful with an abhorrence of all infamous sins against this Commandment, the pastor should have recourse to the Prophets and the other inspired writers, to show the detestation in which God holds the crimes of theft and robbery, and the awful threats which He denounces against their perpetrators. *Hear this*, claims the Prophet Amos, *you that crush the poor, and make the needy of the land to fail, saying: "When will the month be over, and we will sell our wares, and the sabbath, and increase the sickle, and may convey in deceitful balances?"* Many passages of the same kind may be found in Jeremias, Proverbs, and Ecclesiasticus.

Catechism of the Catholic Church (1992)

No. 2408: The seventh commandment forbids theft, that is usurping another's property against the reasonable will of the owner. There is no theft if consent can be presumed or if refusal is contrary to reason and the universal destination of goods. This is the case in obvious and urgent necessity when the only way to provide for immediate essential needs (food, shelter, clothing ...) is to put at one's disposal and use the property of others.

No. 2409: Even if it does not contradict the provisions of civil law, any form of unjustly taking and keeping the property of others is against the seventh commandment: thus, deliberate retention of goods lent or of objects lost; business fraud; paying unjust wages; forcing up prices by taking advantage of the ignorance or hardship of another.

> The following are also morally illicit: speculation in which one contrives to manipulate the price of goods artificially in order to gain an advantage to the detriment of others; corruption in which one influences the judgment of those who must make decisions according to law; appropriation and use for private purposes of the common goods of an enterprise; work poorly done; tax evasion; forgery of checks and invoices; excessive expenses and waste. Willfully damaging private or public property is contrary to the moral law and requires reparation.

No. 2414: The seventh commandment forbids acts or enterprises that for any reason - selfish or ideological, commercial or totalitarian - lead to the enslavement of human beings, to their being bought, sold and exchanged like merchandise, in disregard for their personal dignity. It is a sin against the dignity of persons and their fundamental rights to reduce them by violence to their productive value or to a source of profit. St Paul directed a Christian master to treat his Christian slave "no longer as a slave but more than a slave, as a beloved brother ... both in the flesh and in the Lord."

The Eighth Commandment

"You shall not bear false witness against your neighbor" (Exod. 20:16).

The tongue is the fountainhead from which flows many evils. Hence, the Psalmist says: "Men are all a vain hope" (Ps. 116:11). Conversely, it is a perfect man who has mastered his tongue: "if any one makes no mistakes in what he says he is a perfect man ... So the tongue is a little member and boasts of great things. How great a forest is set ablaze by a small fire!" (Js. 3:2-5).

With regard to this commandment, false testimony is understood as anything positively but falsely affirmed of anyone, be he a neighbor, friend, stranger, enemy, kindred or even himself, be it for or against him, in public or in private. Lies of every sort are condemned: firstly, false testimony given on oath in a court of law; deceit, lying and perjury by all who take part in lawsuits; all testimony which may inflict injury or injustice, wherever given. St Thomas Aquinas states that "lying likens one to the devil" for the devil is "a liar and the father of lies" (Jn 8:44), while St Paul acknowledges the harmful social effects of lying when exhorting the Ephesians to put "away falsehood, let every one speak the truth with his neighbor, for we are members one of another" (Eph. 4:25).

There are three kinds of lies: the jocose lie, one told in jest; the officious lie, a lie told to ward off some evil or to procure some advantage; and the malicious lie, a lie told to expressly injure another. Every lie is essentially opposed to God who gave us the gift of speech to be in accord with our thoughts: "Thou destroyest those who speak lies" (Ps. 5:6); "There are six things which the Lord hates, seven which are an abomination to him: haughty eyes, a lying tongue, and hands that shed innocent blood, a heart that devises wicked plans, feet that make haste to run to evil a false witness who breathes out lies, and a man who sows discord among brothers" (Prov. 6:16-19); "O Lord, who shall sojourn in thy tent? Who shall dwell on thy holy hill? He who walks blamelessly, and does what is right, and speaks truth from his heart; who does not slander with his tongue" (Ps. 15:1). Nevertheless, a lie only amounts to a mortal sin whenever it causes serious injury to our neighbor's goods or honor, or grave scandal. However, to lie in matters of faith is always a mortal sin:

"But false prophets also arose among the people, just as there will be false teachers among you, who will secretly bring in destructive heresies ... And many will follow their licentiousness, and because of them the way of truth will be reviled" (2 Pet. 2:1-2).

Hypocrisy is another species of lie, and consists in trying to esteem ourselves before others by assuming a cloak of virtue, or by pretending to be better than we are. Dissimulation, too, is a lie in action intended to deceive by hiding under a false appearance, and deserves no less to be condemned.

Forbidden also under this commandment is the sin of detraction: "You shall not go up and down as a slanderer among your people" (Lev. 19:16). This involves the action of reviling a person's character, or exaggerating his faults. Likewise, to reveal a person's secret sins or faults without necessity, or to persons who have no right to know, amounts also to detraction: "Do not speak evil against one another, brethren" (Js. 4:11). Neither is it permissible to give a willing ear to a detractor, for if there were no listeners there would be no detractors: "Hedge in your ears with thorns, hear not a wicked tongue" (Sir. 28:28).

To this category can be added those who foment division and quarrels through backbiting and tale bearing. Backbiting is the sin of taking pleasure in speaking of a person's known faults in their absence. To do so in their presence amounts to contumely. Tale bearing is the repeating to a person the unfavorable things that another has said of them. Such a sin often leads to the destruction of peace and harmony among friends and families: "Curse the whisperer and deceiver, for he has destroyed many who were at peace" (Sir. 28:13).

We also injure our neighbor and sin against the eighth commandment when we engage in flattery and insincere praise. Those who seek another's favor, money or honors often stoop to call "evil good, and good evil" (Is. 5:20), praising his sins and causing him to continue in evil and vice. We are called to repel such flatterers from our midst: "Let a good man strike or rebuke me in kindness, but let the oil of the wicked never anoint my head; for my prayer is continually against their wicked deeds" (Ps. 141:5). The most pernicious form of flattery is that which proposes itself to a person in order to lead that person into ruin. Thus, the Jews deceitfully addressed Our Lord: "Teacher, we know that you are true, and teach the way of God truthfully" (Mt 22:16).

Finally, to be avoided is the act of rash judgment when, without sufficient reason or just cause, we think or believe evil of our neighbor. As appearances so often deceive, proof of another's guilt must be solidly founded. Where our neighbor's conduct can bear a favorable interpretation, we should avoid condemnation: "Judge not, that you be not judged" (Mt 7:1).

The Fathers

St Cyril of Jerusalem, *Catechetical Lectures* 1, 5 (c. AD 350)
"Excuse yourself from talking many idle words: neither backbite, nor lend a willing ear to backbiters; but rather be prompt to prayer."

St Jerome, *To Nepotian* Ep. 52 (AD 394)
"Take care not to have an itching tongue, nor tingling ears, that is, neither detract others nor listen to backbiters."

St Augustine of Hippo, *On Lying* 17 (c. AD 395)
"There are two kinds of lie that are not grievously sinful yet are not devoid of sin, when we lie either in joking, or for the sake of our neighbor's good."

St Augustine of Hippo, *The City of God* Bk. 8, C. 20 (ante AD 417)
"To those who do not understand properly, it might seem lawful to give false testimony against one's self, because the words 'against thy neighbor' are subjoined in the Commandment. But let no one who bears false testimony against himself think that he has not violated this Commandment for the standard of loving our neighbor is the love which we cherish towards ourselves."

St Isidore of Seville, *Etymologiae* 10 (c. AD 635)
"The word hypocrite is derived from the appearance of those who come on to the stage with a disguised face, by changing the color of their complexion, so as to imitate the complexion of the person they simulate, at one time under the guise of a man, at another under the guise of a woman, so as to deceive the people in their acting."

The Roman Catechism (1566)

Pt. III, Ch. IX: To all conscientious persons is addressed the divine command that in all their intercourse with society, in every conversation, they should speak the truth at all times from the sincerity of their hearts; that they should utter nothing injurious to the reputation of another, not even of those by whom they know they have been injured and persecuted. For they should always remember that between them and others there exists such a close social bond that they are all members of the same body.

Catechism of the Catholic Church (1992)

No. 2468: Truth as uprightness in human action and speech is called truthfulness, sincerity, or candor. Truth or truthfulness is the virtue which consists in showing oneself true in deeds and truthful in words, and in guarding against duplicity, dissimulation, and hypocrisy.

No. 2477: Respect for the reputation of persons forbids every attitude and word likely to cause them unjust injury. He becomes guilty:

- of rash judgment who, even tacitly, assumes as true without sufficient foundation, the moral fault of a neighbor.
- of detraction who, without objectively valid reason, discloses another's faults and failings to persons who did not know them.
- of calumny who, by remarks contrary to the truth, harms the reputation of others and gives occasion for false judgments concerning them.

The Ninth and Tenth Commandments

"You shall not covet your neighbor's house; you shall not covet your neighbor's wife, or his manservant, or his maidservant, or his ox, or his ass, or anything that is your neighbors" (Exod. 20:17).

What is commanded in these two commandments is the avoidance of covetousness. In them, two different species of covetousness are prohibited (a difference cited by St Augustine of Hippo, *Questions on Exodus*, Qu. 77): one form of covetousness looks to another's spouse for pleasure, while the other to another's goods for profit.

The ninth and tenth commandments shed light on the true understanding and depth of the sixth and seventh commandments. To prohibit the act of adultery, for instance, is also to prohibit its desire, for, were the desire lawful, so too must be its indulgence. Consequently, to fulfil the divine law, not only must there be external observance of duties, but also internal compliance of the heart. Since God reads the heart, we are required to practise purity of heart and maintain sincere integrity of soul: "You have heard that it was said, 'You shall not commit adultery.' But I say to you that every one who looks at a woman lustfully has already committed adultery with her in his heart" (Mt 5:27-28); "man looks on the outward appearance, but the Lord looks on the heart" (1 Sam. 16:7).

At the root of covetousness is concupiscence, which is inherent in our fallen nature. St Thomas Aquinas states that man's desire has no limits, because desire itself is boundless. Excessive and unrestrained desire leads to many kinds of evil: "He who loves money will not be satisfied with money; nor he who loves wealth, with gain: this also is vanity" (Eccles. 5:10). Hence, the need to wage constant combat against ourselves. When freed from cravings of the passions, we are more able to perform our obligations of piety we owe to God: "Thou hast made us for Thyself, O Lord, and our heart is restless until it rests in Thee" (St Augustine of Hippo, *Confessions*, I, 1 [c. AD 400]).

The impulse of concupiscence is not always vicious. The natural well regulated desires for food and drink, warmth and shelter, marital love and sexuality are implanted in us by God and are not prohibited. Lawful concupiscence leads us to continually pray to God for those things which we desire, while the acquisition of the desired good increases our gratitude to God. Furthermore, Scripture itself exhorts us to seek out and desire virtue: "Therefore set your desire on my words" (Wis. 6:11).

St John speaks of three types of concupiscence prohibited to us: "the lust of the flesh and the lust of the eyes and the pride of life" (1 Jn 2:16). They are the source from which all sins flow (Js. 1:14) and all desire contrary to reason and the law of God. Such desire, when consented to, amounts to grievous sin: "Then desire when it has conceived gives birth to sin; and sin when it is full-grown brings forth death" (Js. 1:15).

When the ninth and tenth commandments say, "You shall not covet", they prohibit the desire for those things which belong to others, simply because they belong to another. We are forbidden to thirst for riches or envy the wealth, power, rank or glory of others, or even things of little value whether they are animate or inanimate.

To covet our neighbor's wife is forbidden, together with any desire to marry her. Likewise, it is unlawful to covet another promised in marriage. Furthermore, it is entirely unlawful to desire a virgin consecrated to God: "Turn away your eyes from a shapely woman, and do not look intently at beauty belonging to another" (Sir. 9:8). Unlawful sensual or carnal desire is overcome by avoiding occasions of inappropriate company and idleness, and in engaging in prayer, penance and fasting: "Behold, this was the guilt of your sister Sodom: she and her daughters had pride, surfeit of food, and prosperous ease, but did not aid the poor and needy" (Ezek. 16:49).

The positive part of these commandments enjoins us to detachment and poverty of spirit to the extent that "if riches increase, set not your heart on them" (Ps. 61:10). We should at all times be prepared to sacrifice our goods for the sake of piety, religion, our neighbor or the poor. If poverty is our lot, we should bear it with patience and resignation. To be generous with our own goods is a sure means of extinguishing the flames of covetousness. Added to this, our desires should be directed to know and fulfill the will of God for ourselves, along a virtuous road of life.

The Fathers

St Augustine of Hippo, *On Free Choice* Bk. 3, 3 (c. AD 395)
"Covetousness applies not only to silver or money, but also to anything that is desired immoderately."

St Augustine of Hippo, *Corrections* I, 15 (c. AD 427)
"Concupiscence is the guilt of original sin."

St Gregory the Great, *Homilies on Ezekiel* 16 (AD 593)
"Covetousness is a desire not only for money, but also for knowledge and high places, when prominence is immoderately sought after."

St Gregory the Great, *Moral Teachings from the Book of Job* Bk. 15 (AD 595)
"Covetousness arises sometimes from pride, sometimes from fear. For there are those who, when they think that they lack the needful for their expenses, allow the mind to give way to covetousness. And there are others who, wishing to be thought more of, are incited to greed for other people's property."

St Isidore of Seville, *Commentary on Deuteronomy* (ante AD 636)
(There are nine daughters of covetousness) "lying, fraud, theft, perjury, greed of filthy lucre, false witnessing, violence, inhumanity, rapacity."

The Roman Catechism (1566)

Pt. III, Ch. X: By the preceding Commandments God had, as it were, fenced us round with safeguards, securing us and ours against injury of every sort; but by the addition of these two Commandments, He intended chiefly to provide against the injuries which we might inflict on ourselves by the indulgence of inordinate desires, as would easily happen were we at liberty to covet all things indiscriminately. By this law then, which forbids to covet, God has blunted in some degree the keenness of desire, which excites to every kind of evil, so that by reason of His command these desires are to some extent diminished, and we ourselves, freed from the annoying importunity of the passions, are enabled to devote more time to the performance of the numerous and important duties of piety and religion which we owe to God.

Catechism of the Catholic Church (1992)

No. 2514: St John distinguishes three kinds of covetousness or concupiscence: lust of the flesh, lust of the eyes, and pride of life. In Catholic catechetical tradition, the ninth commandment forbids carnal concupiscence; the tenth forbids coveting another's goods.

No. 2517: The heart is the seat of moral personality: "out of the heart come evil thoughts, murder, adultery, fornication ..." The struggle against carnal covetousness entails purifying the heart and practising temperance:

> Remain simple and innocent, and you will be like little children who do not know the evil that destroys man's life (*Shepherd of Hermas*, Mandate 2, 1).

No. 2534: The tenth commandment unfolds and completes the ninth, which is concerned with concupiscence of the flesh. It forbids coveting the goods of another, as the root of theft, robbery, and fraud, which the seventh commandment forbids. "Lust of the eyes" leads to the violence and injustice forbidden by the fifth commandment. Avarice, like fornication, originates in the idolatry prohibited by the first three prescriptions of the Law. The tenth commandment concerns the intentions of the heart; with the ninth, it summarizes all the precepts of the Law.

Part III

The Lord's Prayer

Introduction

"Let my prayer be counted as incense before thee, and the lifting up of my hands as an evening sacrifice!" (Ps. 141:2).

Our Lord Jesus Christ while on earth often spent time in prayer, occasionally for a whole day and night together (Mk 1:35; Lk 9:29). If Our Lord Himself needed to pray, how much more do we. Prayer is essentially communicating with God as children to a loving Father, the raising of our hearts and minds to Him. Part of Our Lord's great mission was to teach us how to pray: "Lord, teach us to pray" (Lk 11:1).

Our Lord speaks on prayer throughout the Gospels. Essentially, Christ taught that prayer should be:

(i) Unselfish (Mt 6:9).
(ii) Strong and constant (Lk 18:1-7).
(iii) Humble (Lk 18:9).
(iv) Sincere (Mk 9:25).
(v) Trusting (Mt 7:8-11).
(vi) United to Him (Jn 14:13).

The following Scriptural passages further illustrate these points:

"And he said to them, 'Which of you who has a friend will go to him at midnight and say to him, Friend, lend me three loaves; for a friend of mine has arrived on a journey, and I have nothing to set before him; and he will answer from within, Do not bother me; the door is now shut, and my children are with me in bed; I cannot get up and give you anything? I tell you, though he will not get up and give him anything because he is his friend, yet because of his importunity he will rise and give him whatever he needs. And I tell you, Ask, and it will be given you; seek, and you will find; knock, and it will be opened to you. For every one who asks receives, and he who seeks finds, and to him who knocks it will be opened'" (Lk 11:5-10).

"Let us then with confidence draw near to the throne of grace, that we may receive mercy and find grace to help in time of need" (Heb. 4:16).

"But let him ask in faith, with no doubting, for he who doubts is like a wave of the sea that is driven and tossed by the wind" (Js. 1:6).

"You ask and do not receive, because you ask wrongly, to spend it on your passions" (Js. 4:3).

In addition to faith and perseverance in prayer, God also may require penance:

"And Jesus answered, 'O faithless and perverse generation, how long am I to be with you? How long am I to bear with you? Bring him here to me.' And Jesus rebuked him, and the demon came out of him, and the boy was cured instantly. Then the disciples came to Jesus privately and said, 'Why could we not cast it out?' He said to them, 'Because of your little faith. For truly, I say to you, if you have faith as a grain of mustard seed, you will say to this mountain, Move from here to there, and it will move; and nothing will be impossible to you'" (Mt 17:17-20).

There are times when we do not receive from God what we ask for. This could be due to our own sin, pride or negligence (Mt 20:20; Lk 12:13), or because we ask for things which are prejudicial to our welfare and salvation. No prayer in fact is ever left unanswered, it may simply be that the answer is no.

Being creatures of God who are entirely dependent upon Him for all our needs, daily prayer should encompass all of the following aspects:

(i) Adoration of God.
(ii) Thanksgiving for benefits received.
(iii) Asking pardon for sins committed.
(iv) Petition for spiritual and temporal needs.

In this order we place God's glory and honor first, and our particular needs second. The correct order concerning our needs is that we should prefer spiritual and heavenly things to those merely bodily and earthly: *"But seek first his kingdom and his righteousness, and all these things shall be yours as well"* (Mt 6:33).

Introduction

No prayer better expresses what we should pray for and the order in which we should pray for them than the very prayer Our Lord taught us:

"Our Father who art in heaven,
Hallowed be thy name.
Thy Kingdom come,
Thy will be done
On earth as it is in heaven.
Give us this day our daily bread;
And forgive us our debts, as we also have forgiven our debtors;
And lead us not into temptation,
But deliver us from evil" (Mt 6:9-13).

Likewise:

"He was praying in a certain place, and when he ceased, one of his disciples said to him, 'Lord, teach us to pray, as John taught his disciples.' And he said to them, 'When you pray, say:

Father,
hallowed be thy name.
Thy kingdom come.
Give us each day our daily bread;
and forgive us our sins,
for we ourselves forgive every one who is indebted to us;
and lead us not into temptation'" (Lk 11:1-4).

This prayer, more commonly known as the "Our Father", is made up, in Matthew's Gospel, of an opening address plus seven petitions. It is considered the most important of all the Church's prayers, and is used extensively both in public and private worship. Whatever we could ever properly ask for is contained in this prayer. As St Augustine of Hippo says, "we cannot but utter that which is contained in Our Lord's prayer, if we pray in a suitable and worthy manner" (*To Proba*, Ep. 130 AD 412).

The Fathers

The Didache 8, 2 (inter AD 90-150)
"Do not pray as the hypocrites do, but as the Lord commanded in His gospel, you shall pray thus: Our Father who art in heaven, hallowed be thy name. Thy kingdom come, thy will be done on earth, as it is in heaven. Give us this day our daily bread, and forgive us our debts, as we also forgive our debtors. And lead us not into temptation, but deliver us from evil. For thine is the power and the glory forever. Pray thus three times a day."

St Cyprian of Carthage, *The Lord's Prayer* 3 (c. AD 251-252)
"Since we have Christ as our Advocate with the Father for our sins, when we pray on account of our faults, we use the very words of our Advocate."

St Jerome, *Commentaries on the Gospel of St Matthew* 7, 4 (AD 398)
"Every one that asks, receives, as it is written. If, therefore, it is not given you, this is because you do not ask. Ask, therefore, and you shall receive."

St John Chrysostom, *Homilies on Prayer* II (ante AD 407)
"Think what happiness is granted you, what honor bestowed upon you, when you converse with God in prayer, when you talk with Christ, when you ask what you will, whatever you desire."

St John Chrysostom, *Selection on Prayer* 2 (ante AD 407)
"It is possible to offer fervent prayer even while walking in public or strolling alone, or seated in your shop, ... while buying or selling, ... or even while cooking."

St Augustine of Hippo, *To Proba* Ep. 130, 12 (AD 412)
"The Lord's Prayer is the most perfect of prayers, because if we pray aright we can say naught else save what is set down in that Prayer. For prayer is in some sort the expression before God of our desires; consequently we can only rightly ask in our prayers for what we can rightly desire. Now in the Lord's Prayer we not only find all the petitions that we can rightly desire to make, but they are set down in the very order in which we ought

to desire them, so that this Prayer not only teaches us how to ask but serves as a guide to all our desires."

The Roman Catechism (1566)

Pt. IV, Ch. I: Prayer is a duty not only recommended by way of counsel, but also commanded by obligatory precept. Christ the Lord declared this when He said: *We should pray always ...*

The first fruit which we receive is that by praying we honor God, since prayer is a certain act of religion, which is compared in Scripture to a sweet perfume. *Let my prayer*, says the Prophet, *be directed as incense in thy sight.* By prayer we confess our subjection to God; we acknowledge and proclaim Him to be the author of all good, in whom alone we center all our hopes, who alone is our refuge, in all dangers and the bulwark of our salvation.

Catechism of the Catholic Church (1992)

No. 2559: "Prayer is the raising of one's mind and heart to God or the requesting of good things from God." But when we pray, do we speak from the height of our pride and will, or "out of the depths" of a humble and contrite heart? He who humbles himself will be exalted; humility is the foundation of prayer. Only when we humbly acknowledge that "we do not know how to pray as we ought", we are ready to receive freely the gift of prayer. "Man is a beggar before God."

No. 2750: By entering into the holy name of the Lord Jesus we can accept, from within, the prayer he teaches us: "Our Father!" his priestly prayer fulfills, from within, the great petitions of the Lord's Prayer: concern for the Father's name; passionate zeal for his kingdom (glory); the accomplishment of the will of the Father, of his plan of salvation; and deliverance from evil.

Our Father who art in Heaven

"For you did not receive the spirit of slavery to fall back into fear, but you have received the spirit of sonship. When we cry, 'Abba! Father'" (Rom. 8:15).

Our Lord Jesus Christ, in composing and giving us His prayer, began by addressing God in such terms so as to inspire in us love and confidence. No longer were we to approach God as timid and fearful servants. For what could inspire us more to pray than to know that we are about to address a God who is a loving and tender Father?

God is appropriately called Father by virtue of having created man to His own image and likeness and redeeming him from his iniquities: "Is not he your father, who created you, who made you and established you?" (Deut. 32:6). Though mankind has offended God through countless crimes, God has never renounced His special love and solicitude for us: "in wrath remember mercy" (Hab. 3:2). God at all times preserves us by His special providence and provides for all our needs: "but it is thy providence, O Father, that steers its course ... showing that thou canst save from every danger" (Wis. 14:3-4).

St Thomas Aquinas states that as our Father we owe God four things. Firstly, honor: "If then I am a father, where is my honor?" (Mal. 1:6); secondly, imitation: "And I thought you would call me, 'My Father', and would not turn from following me" (Jer. 3:19); thirdly, obedience: "Shall we not much more be subject to the Father of spirits and live?" (Heb. 12:9); and, finally, patience in chastisement: "My son, do not despise the Lord's discipline or be weary of his reproof, for the Lord reproves him whom he loves" (Prov. 3:11-12).

Above all the acts of God's creation, providence and mercy, shines His redemption of man. By justice alone, man deserved to be left in a miserable state, cast out of Paradise, subject to toil, suffering and death, and excluded from God's grace and heaven. Yet, God, in an act of His mercy unmerited by man deigned to send His Only-Begotten Son to redeem the world through His passion and death. By this act of redemption, man is restored to the sonship of God: "he gave power to become children of God" (Jn 1:12). Furthermore, by baptism God bestows upon us the gift of His Holy Spirit to seal our adoption as sons of God: "For you did not receive the spirit of slavery to fall back into fear, but you have received the spirit of sonship. When we cry, 'Abba! Father'" (Rom. 8:15).

By addressing God as "Our" Father, the faithful show their unity as adopted sons of God in one brotherhood united to Christ: "and he has put all things under his feet and has made him the head over all things for the church, which is his body" (Eph. 1:22-23). Being true man, Christ is truly our brother and the head of this brotherhood, the source of our sanctification: "For he who sanctifies and those who are sanctified have all one origin. That is why he is not ashamed to call them brethren" (Heb. 2:11).

As one body addressing the same Father, Christians ought to be mindful to pray not only for their own needs, but also for those of the whole Church of God. This is done by sincerely uttering the word "Our." Prayer for others out of fraternal charity is inspired by grace and is more agreeable to God than only prayer for ourselves. The bonds of brotherhood also oblige us to be ever respectful and charitable to others, seeking always their good welfare and never attempting to pursue our own ends at another's expense: "For as many of you as were baptized into Christ have put on Christ. There is neither Jew nor Greek, there is neither slave nor free, there is neither male nor female; for you are all one in Christ Jesus" (Gal. 3:27-28).

"Who art in heaven" pertains to God who is enthroned above upon His high sanctuary. Scripture speaks specifically of heaven as His dwelling-place: "If I ascend to heaven, thou art there!" (Ps. 139:8). However, God being pure spirit is indivisible and therefore present in all places and to all things without limit, beholding all in His survey of us: "that he looked down from his holy height, from heaven the Lord looked at the earth" (Ps. 102:19). "In heaven" are also appropriate words in prayer for they direct our minds to focus on that spiritual and eternal good which is our true end: "Set your minds on things that are above" (Col. 3:2). It is in heaven that God reigns enthroned with Christ at His right-hand, where the angels bestow unto Him unceasing praise, and those who are found worthy of His kingdom behold Him face to face.

The Fathers

Tertullian, *On Prayer* 1, 3 (inter AD 200-206)
"The prayer begins with a confession of belief in God and a merit-bearing act of faith, as we say, 'Father, who art in heaven.' For this form of address results when we adore God and affirm our faith. It is written, 'To those who believe in God, he gave the power to be called children of God.' Our Lord often spoke to us of God as a Father. Indeed, he taught us to call no one on earth 'father', but the one who is Father in heaven. Thus, when we pray in this manner, we are also obedient to the Lord's precept. Happy are they who know their Father! ... The expression God the Father had never been revealed to anyone. When Moses himself asked God who He was, He heard another name. The Father's name has been revealed to us in the Son, for the name 'Son' implies the new name 'Father.'"

St Cyril of Jerusalem, *Catechetical Lectures* 23, 11 (c. AD 350)
"Then, after these things, we say that prayer which the Savior imparted to His own disciples; and with pure conscience we describe God as Father, saying: "Our Father who art in heaven." Oh, how great is the loving-kindness of God! On those who have defected from Him, and who were in the extremities of wickedness, He has bestowed such an amnesty for the wicked deeds and so great a sharing in grace that they may even call Him Father: Our Father who art in heaven. But they too are a heaven who bear the likeness of the heavenly, in whom is God, dwelling and walking about."

St John Chrysostom, *Homilies on the Gospel of St Matthew*, Hom. 14 (c. AD 390)
"God listens willingly to the Christian who prays not only for himself but for others; because to pray for ourselves is an inspiration of nature; but to pray for others is an inspiration of grace; necessity compels us to pray for ourselves, whereas fraternal charity calls on us to pray for others."

Law and Life

St Augustine of Hippo, *The Lord's Sermon on the Mount in Matthew* 2, 4 (inter AD 392-396)
"Our Father: at this name love is aroused in us ... and the confidence of obtaining what we are about to ask ... What would He not give to His children who ask, since He has already granted them the gift of being His children?"

The Roman Catechism (1566)

Pt. IV, Ch. IX: Our Savior could, indeed, have commenced this divine prayer with some other word, conveying more the idea of majesty, such, for instance, as *Lord* or *Creator*. Yet He omitted all such expressions because they might rather inspire fear, and instead of them He has chosen a term inspiring confidence and love in those who pray and ask anything of God; for what is sweeter than the name *Father*, conveying, as it does, the idea of indulgence and tenderness?

Catechism of the Catholic Church (1992)

No. 2780: We can invoke God as "Father" because *he is revealed to us* by his Son become man and because his Spirit makes him known to us. The personal relation of the Son to the Father is something that man cannot conceive of nor the angelic powers even dimly see: and yet, the Spirit of the Son grants a participation in that very relation to us who believe that Jesus is the Christ and that we are born of God.

No. 2792: Finally, if we pray the Our Father sincerely, we leave individualism behind, because the love that we receive frees us from it. The "our" at the beginning of the Lord's Prayer, like the "us" of the last four petitions, excludes no one. If we are to say it truthfully, our divisions and oppositions have to be overcome.

Hallowed be Thy Name

"'Father, glorify thy name.' Then a voice came from heaven, 'I have glorified it, and I will glorify it again'" (Jn 12:28).

Genuine and well-ordered piety directs us to honor and worship God as the supreme good first and above all other things. Hence, in the Lord's Prayer, we turn our thoughts towards honoring the name of God before asking of Him anything for others or ourselves.

By "name" is meant the honor that a person is held in. When we hallow God's name, we mean to increase the reverence and glory given to it and desire that it be better and more extensively known, and that through such knowledge God's kingdom and holy will may triumph and be obeyed throughout the world: "As thy name, O God, so thy praise reaches to the ends of the earth" (Ps. 48:10). Furthermore, where the name of God is ignored, dishonored or blasphemed, appropriate reparation may be made to appease the divine justice: "Who shall not fear and glorify thy name, O Lord?" (Rev. 15:4).

Any honor given to God's Name on earth will always be far short of what He truly and properly deserves. This is because His name is already "Holy and terrible" (Ps. 111:9) and no creature can increase the holiness of a name which already possesses all holiness in an infinite degree from all eternity. Nevertheless, in union with the heavenly hosts who unceasingly give Him praise, we are exhorted to proclaim the holiness of the name of God interiorly and exteriorly with mind, body and soul: "Bless the Lord, O my soul; and all that is within me, bless his holy name!" (Ps. 103:1).

However, unlike the angels in heaven, not all on earth know and praise the name of the true God. Implicitly, when we hallow the name of God we pray that all on earth may do likewise, and that the nations in ignorance be converted and that sinners be restored to their former holiness: "I will not let my holy name be profaned any more; and the nations shall know that I am the Lord, the Holy One in Israel" (Ezek. 39:7). In addition, it is our prayer that all alike recognize the beneficence of God, and that all good things, natural and supernatural, are blessings from His ever-generous hands: "for he who is mighty has done great things for me, and holy is his name" (Lk 1:49).

Together with the name of God Himself, the name of Jesus should be equally hallowed, for He is the God-man whose name is the only "name under heaven given among men by which we must be saved" (Acts 4:12). At the name of Jesus "every knee should bow, in heaven and on earth and under the earth" (Phil. 2:10). Through Our Lord's name, man can work many wonders: "... in my name they will cast out demons; they will speak in new tongues; they will pick up serpents, and if they drink any deadly thing, it will not hurt them; they will lay their hands on the sick, and they will recover" (Mk 16:17-18).

Along with praising the name of God in word we are called upon more so to praise His name in deed: "Well did Isaiah prophesy of you hypocrites, as it is written, 'This people honors me with their lips, but their heart is far from me'" (Mk 7:6). For the evil deeds of the faithful are imputed to the Author of religion by the ignorant or those opposed to the Church: "The name of God is blasphemed among the Gentiles because of you" (Rom. 2:24). Contrariwise, those who live faithfully and regulate their lives in word and deed lead others to praise the name of God: "Let your light so shine before men, that they may see your good works and give glory to your Father who is in heaven" (Mt 5:16).

The Fathers

Tertullian, *On Prayer* 3 (inter AD 200-206)
"When we ask 'hallowed be thy name,' we ask that it should be hallowed in us, who are in Him; but also in others whom God's grace still awaits, that we may obey the precept that obliges us to pray for everyone, even our enemies. That is why we do not say expressly 'hallowed be thy name in us', for we ask that it be so in all men."

St Cyprian of Carthage, *The Lord's Prayer* 12 (c. AD 251-252)
"After this we say: 'Hallowed be thy name', not that we want God to be made holy by our prayers, but because we seek from the Lord that His name may be made holy in us. Indeed, by whom could God be made holy, when it is He that sanctifies? But because He Himself said, 'Be holy, as I too am holy', we ask and seek that very thing, so that we who have

been made holy in Baptism may persevere in what we have begun to be. For this we pray daily. We have a daily need of being made holy, so that we who sin daily may be cleansed again of our sins by continual sanctification."

St Cyril of Jerusalem, *Catechetical Lectures* **23, 12 (c. AD 350)**
"Hallowed be thy name: – which for all our saying or not saying, the name of God is by nature holy. But since it is sometimes profaned among sinners, according to the saying, 'Through you My name is continually blasphemed among the gentiles', we pray that among us the name of God may be hallowed: not that from not being holy it may become holy, but that it may become holy among us, by our being made holy and by our doing deeds worthy of holiness."

St Gregory of Nyssa, *The Lord's Prayer* **3 (inter AD 371-395)**
"Who is so bereft of the finer sensibilities as not, on beholding the spotless life of believers, to glorify the name that is invoked by those who lead such a life?"

St Augustine of Hippo, *The Lord's Sermon on the Mount in Matthew* **2, 5 (inter AD 392-396)**
"We do not mean to imply that the name of God is not holy, but we ask that it may be regarded by all men as holy; that is, that God may become so well known that men will not judge anything to be holier."

St Peter Chrysologus, *Sermons* **71, 4 (post AD 432)**
"We ask God to hallow His name, which by its own holiness saves and makes holy all creation ... It is this name that gives salvation to a lost world. But we ask that this name of God should be hallowed in us through our actions. For God's name is blessed when we live well, but is blasphemed when we live wickedly."

The Roman Catechism (1566)

Pt. IV, Ch. X: Thus we desire and beg that His name may be more and better known in the world, that His kingdom may be extended, and that each day new servants may come to obey His holy will. These three things, His name, His kingdom, and obedience (to His will), do not appertain to the intrinsic nature and perfection of God, but are extrinsic thereto.

Catechism of the Catholic Church (1992)

No. 2807: The term "to hallow" is to be understood here not primarily in its causative sense (only God hallows, makes holy), but above all in an evaluative sense: to recognize as holy, to treat in a holy way. And so, in adoration, this invocation is sometimes understood as praise and thanksgiving. But this petition is here taught to us by Jesus as an optative: a petition, a desire, and an expectation in which God and man are involved. Beginning with this first petition to our Father, we are immersed in the innermost mystery of his Godhead and the drama of the salvation of our humanity. Asking the Father that his name be made holy draws us into his plan of loving kindness for the fullness of time, "according to his purpose which he set forth in Christ", that we might " be holy and blameless before him in love."

Thy Kingdom Come

"The time is fulfilled, and the kingdom of God is at hand; repent, and believe in the gospel" (Mk 1:15).

In this petition we seek of God the coming of His kingdom, both in the world and in ourselves. The theme of God's kingdom and its coming was central in the mission of Our Lord Jesus Christ: "I must preach the good news of the kingdom of God to the other cities also; for I was sent for this purpose" (Lk 4:43); "for you, go and proclaim the kingdom of God" (Lk 9:60).

By the kingdom of God we first understand it to mean the manifestation of that power which God possesses to rule all men and all things. Our love for God should compel us to pray that His reign may be manifest "awaiting our blessed hope, the appearing of the glory of our great God and Savior" (Tit. 2:13). In acknowledgment of His power, God should be publicly worshipped by all peoples and in all places: "May all kings fall down before him, all nations serve him!" (Ps. 72:11). Consequently, the laws, institutions and customs of every society should be based on Christian principles, with Christ as king: "Of the increase of his government and of peace there will be no end, upon the throne of David, and over his kingdom, to establish it, and to uphold it with justice and with righteousness from this time forth and for evermore. The zeal of the Lord of hosts will do this" (Is. 9:7).

Yet, Our Lord declared before Pilate "my kingship is not from the world" (Jn 18:36). Nor is it a kingdom whose coming shall be visible to the children of this world: "The kingdom of God is not coming with signs to be observed; nor will they say, 'Lo, here it is!' or 'There!'" (Lk 17:20-21). Instead, "the kingdom of God is not food and drink but righteousness and peace and joy in the Holy Spirit" (Rom. 14:17). Christ invisibly reigns in the souls of the just by sanctifying grace: "If a man loves me, he will keep my word, and my Father will love him, and we will come to him and make our home with him" (Jn 14:23).

Without this interior kingdom of grace no one can enter into God's kingdom of glory: "... no fornicator or impure man, or one who is covetous (that is, an idolater), has any inheritance in the kingdom of

Christ and of God" (Eph. 5:5). This kingdom, the kingdom of heaven, is the eternal reward awaiting the just: "Come, O blessed of my Father, inherit the kingdom prepared for you from the foundation of the world" (Mt 25:34). It is indescribable: "... no eye has seen, nor ear heard, nor the heart of man conceived, what God has prepared for those who love him" (1 Cor. 2:9). All the faithful ought to strive to the utmost and sacrifice all to acquire this kingdom: "a man found and covered up; then in his joy he goes and sells all that he has and buys that field" (Mt 13:44). Then shall all that is defiled and unsuitable be entirely removed and all weakness strengthened: "flesh and blood cannot inherit the kingdom of God, nor does the perishable inherit the imperishable" (1 Cor. 15:50).

When we pray that God's kingdom "come", we pray that God alone may reign as the true and only God of all and that the power of God's enemies be broken. This is not yet the case, but will be so at the end of the world: "For he must reign until he has put all his enemies under his feet" (1 Cor. 15:25). Furthermore, we pray that the Church extend her dominion over the entire earth, that pagans and unbelievers be converted, and that those in error or schism be restored to full communion under the one shepherd: "And nations shall come to your light, and kings to the brightness of your rising. Lift up your eyes round about, and see; they all gather together, they come to you; your sons shall come from far, and your daughters shall be carried in the arms" (Is. 60:3-4).

We also pray for the return of Our Lord to judge the living and the dead, to destroy death, to consummate all things and to be glorified before all: "When the Son of man comes in his glory, and all the angels with him, then he will sit on his glorious throne. Before him will be gathered all the nations, and he will separate them one from another ... And they will go away into eternal punishment, but the righteous into eternal life" (Mt 25:31-46).

Finally, we pray for God's continual assistance, to maintain us in a state of grace and guide us along the path that leads to heaven: "Search me, O God, and know my heart! Try me and know my thoughts! And see if there be any wicked way in me, and lead me in the way everlasting!" (Ps. 139:23-24).

The Fathers

Tertullian, *On Prayer* 5 (inter AD 200-206)
"Even if it had not been prescribed to pray for the coming of the kingdom, we would willingly have brought forth this speech, eager to embrace our hope. In indignation the souls of the martyrs under the altar cry out to the Lord ... For their retribution is ordained for the end of the world. Indeed, as soon as possible, Lord, may your kingdom come!"

St Cyprian of Carthage, *The Lord's Prayer* 13 (c. AD 251-252)
"There follows in the prayer, Thy kingdom come. We ask that the kingdom of God may be set forth to us, even as we also ask that His name may be sanctified in us. For when does God not reign, or when does that begin with Him which both always has been, and never ceases to be? We pray that our kingdom, which has been promised us by God, may come, which was acquired by the blood and passion of Christ; that we who first are His subjects in the world, may hereafter reign with Christ when He reigns, as He Himself promises ... Christ Himself, dearest brethren, however, may be the kingdom of God, whom we day by day desire to come, whose advent we crave to be quickly manifested to us. For since He is Himself the Resurrection, since in Him we rise again, so also the kingdom of God may be understood to be Himself, since in Him we shall reign. But we do well in seeking the kingdom of God, that is, the heavenly kingdom, because there is also an earthly kingdom. But he who has already renounced the world, is moreover greater than its honors and its kingdom. And therefore he who dedicates himself to God and Christ, desires not earthly, but heavenly kingdoms."

St Cyril of Jerusalem, *Catechetical Lectures* 23, 13 (c. AD 350)
"It is the privilege of a pure soul to say with holiness: 'Thy kingdom come.' He that has heard Paul say, 'Let not, therefore, sin reign in your mortal body,' and has cleansed himself in deed and in thought and in word will say to God, 'Thy kingdom come'."

St Gregory of Nyssa, *The Lord's Prayer* 3 (inter AD 371-395)
"Thy Kingdom come. By this sweet word we obviously offer God this prayer: Let the opposing battlefront be broken and the hostile phalanx be destroyed. Bring to an end the war of the flesh against the spirit and let the body no longer harbor the enemy of the soul. Oh, let them appear, the royal force, the angelic band, the thousands of rulers, the myriads of those who stand on Thy right hand, that a thousand warriors may fall on the front of the enemy! Strong, indeed, is the adversary, formidable, yea, invincible to those bereft of Thy help. Yet only as long as man is fighting alone; when Thy Kingdom comes, the pangs and sighs of sorrow vanish, and life, peace, and rejoicing enter instead."

The Roman Catechism (1566)

Pt. IV, Ch. XI: ... let us then implore the Spirit of God that He may command us to do all things in accordance with His holy will; that He may so overthrow the empire of Satan that it shall have no power over us on the great accounting day; that Christ may be victorious and triumphant; that the divine influence of His law may be spread throughout the world; that His ordinances may be observed; that there be found no traitor, no deserter; and that all may so conduct themselves, as to come with joy into the celestial kingdom, prepared for them from all eternity, in the fruition of endless bliss with Christ Jesus.

Catechism of the Catholic Church (1992)

No. 2816: In the New Testament, the word basileia can be translated by "kingship" (abstract noun), "kingdom" (concrete noun) or "reign" (action noun). The Kingdom of God lies ahead of us. It is brought near in the Word incarnate, it is proclaimed throughout the whole Gospel, and it has come in Christ's death and Resurrection. The Kingdom of God has been coming since the Last Supper and, in the Eucharist, it is in our midst. The kingdom will come in glory when Christ hands it over to his Father
...

No. 2818: In the Lord's Prayer, "thy kingdom come" refers primarily to the final coming of the reign of God through Christ's return. But, far from distracting the Church from her mission in this present world, this desire commits her to it all the more strongly. Since Pentecost, the coming of that Reign is the work of the Spirit of the Lord who "complete(s) his work on earth and brings us the fullness of grace."

Thy Will be Done

"For whoever does the will of my Father in heaven is my brother, and sister, and mother" (Mt 12:50).

Our salvation is dependent upon seeking the will of God and fulfilling it: "Not every one who says to me, 'Lord, Lord,' shall enter the kingdom of heaven, but he who does the will of my Father who is in heaven" (Mt 7:21); "And that servant who knew his master's will, but did not make ready or act according to his will, shall receive a severe beating" (Lk 12:47). Hence, those who put their trust in their own knowledge and judgment without reference to God's will are accounted to be foolish and proud: "Do you see a man who is wise in his own eyes? There is more hope for a fool than for him" (Prov. 26:12). The heart of man can only be at peace when it is in accord with the will of God: "Thou hast made us for Thyself, O Lord, and our heart is restless until it rests in Thee."[1]

Christ Himself set the example of obedience to God's will when declaring "I have come down from heaven, not to do my own will, but the will of him who sent me" (Jn 6:38). Also, beholding in the Garden of Gethsemani the sufferings He was about to endure for our salvation, Christ denied Himself and declared "not as I will, but as thou wilt" (Mt 26:39). To fulfil the will of God in ourselves requires constant self-denial, crucifying our own will, pride and concupiscence: "If any man would come after me, let him deny himself and take up his cross and follow me" (Mt 16:24). Yet, with joy should we seek to fulfil God's will, the same joy Our Lady herself expressed when giving the Angel Gabriel her fiat: "Behold, I am the handmaid of the Lord; let it be to me according to your word" (Lk 1:38).

Nothing is more pleasing to God than readiness to obey His holy will, and great are the rewards He bestows on those who fulfil it: "If you turn back your foot from the sabbath, from doing your pleasure on my holy day ... I will make you ride upon the heights of the earth; I will feed you with the heritage of Jacob your father, for the mouth of the Lord has spoken" (Is. 58:13-14); "he who does the will of God abides for ever" (1

---

[1] St Augustine of Hippo, *Confessions*, I, 1 (c. AD 400).

Jn 2:17). Furthermore, to do the will of the Father is to be identified most intimately with Christ Himself: "For whoever does the will of my Father in heaven is my brother and sister and mother" (Mt 12:50).

St Thomas Aquinas states that God wills of us three things: firstly, that we have eternal life: "For this is the will of my Father, that every one who sees the Son and believes in him should have eternal life" (Jn 6:40); secondly, that we keep His commandments: "If you would enter life, keep the commandments" (Mt 19:17); thirdly, that men be restored to the original state of integrity in which the spirit and soul dominated sensuality and the flesh: "For the desires of the flesh are against the Spirit" (Gal. 5:17). We therefore should pray that God may give us the grace to fulfil all our obligations, together with the strength never to depart the path of holiness.

Our willingness to know and abide by the will of God should be akin to that of the angels of heaven, who are "his ministers that do his will" (Ps. 103:21). This is implied in the appendix to this petition that states "on earth as it is in heaven." The angels willingly and joyfully obey God's will, free from all motives except pure love of God. God's will on earth will finally be done as it is in heaven when Christ returns to judge the living and the dead. In the meantime, we should pray that the world at large may come to know God's will.

In our prayers we should ask that God's will for us be always fulfilled, particularly with respect to knowing and carrying out our vocations. At the same time, we should endeavor to avoid praying for those things that are unworthy, or dangerous for our salvation. Even in the case where the object of our desire is objectively good we should always conclude our prayer with the words "thy will be done." Where we are vexed by tribulation, sickness, persecution or suffering of any kind we should acquiesce to God's permissive will, fortifying ourselves with the words of Job: "Naked I came from my mother's womb, and naked shall I return; the Lord gave, and the Lord has taken away; blessed be the name of the Lord" (Job 1:21).

The Fathers

Tertullian, *On Prayer* 4 (inter AD 200-206)
"Following this, we add: 'thy will be done in heaven and on earth.' We are not praying because someone actually could prevent the accomplishment of God's will or as if our prayers could assure its fulfilment. Rather, we pray for God's will to be done in everyone. Through symbolic interpretation, we understand that we, flesh and spirit, are heaven and earth. If, however, we are to take these words straightforwardly, the sense of this petition is the same: that the will of God may be done in us, on earth, certainly so that it may also be done in the same way, in heaven. Now, what does God will more than that we walk along the way he has taught us? We ask, then, that the substance and the resources of his will be supplied to us, that we might be saved both in heaven and earth. For the fullness of his will is that those he has adopted as children be saved."

Origen, *On Prayer* 26 (post AD 231)
"We who pray while we are still on earth must understand that the will of God is done in heaven by all who are there with God. Let us, then, pray that his will be done by us on earth, in all things, just as it is done by those who are in heaven. This will happen if we do nothing opposed to the will of God. When God's will is done on earth by us as it is in heaven, then shall we be like those who are in heaven: we, too, shall bear the image of the heavenly bodies; we shall be heirs to the kingdom of heaven. Those who come after us, while they are still on earth, will pray to be like us, for we shall then be in heaven."

St Cyprian of Carthage, *The Lord's Prayer* 14 (c. AD 251-252)
"We continue and say: 'Thy will be done on earth as it is in heaven', not as if praying that God may do as He wills, but that we may be able to do what God wills: for who could withstand God and prevent His doing what He wills! But since the devil withstands us, and would prevent our thoughts and deeds from being devoted in all things to obedience to God, we pray and petition that God's will be done in us. And in order that it might be done in us we have need of God's will, that is, of His help

and protection, since no one is strong by his own powers, but is safe only by the kindliness and mercy of God."

St Cyril of Jerusalem, *Catechetical Lectures* **23, 14 (c. AD 350)**
"Thy will be done on earth as it is in heaven. The divine and blessed angels of God do the will of God, as David says when He sings, 'Bless the Lord, all you His angels, you that are mighty in strength, doing the things He wills.' In effect, then, in so praying, you say, 'As Your will is done in the angels, Master, so also let it be done on earth in me.'"

St John Chrysostom, *Homilies on the Gospel of St Matthew* **Hom. 19, 5 (c. AD 390)**
"For he did not say 'thy will be done in me or in us', but 'on earth,' the whole earth, so that error may be banished from it, truth take root in it, all vice be destroyed on it, virtue flourish on it, and earth no longer differ from heaven."

The Roman Catechism (1566)

Pt. IV, Ch. XII: Now this is what we ask when we address to God these words: *Thy will be done.* We fell into this state of misery by disobeying and despising the divine will. God vouchsafes to propose to us, as the sole corrective of such great evils, a conformity to His will, which by sinning we despised; He commands us to regulate all our thoughts and actions by this standard. Now it is precisely His help to accomplish this that we ask when we suppliantly address to God the prayer, *Thy will be done.*

Catechism of the Catholic Church (1992)

No. 2822: Our Father "desires all men to be saved and to come to the knowledge of the truth." He "is forbearing toward you, not wishing that any should perish." His commandment is "that you love one another; even as I have loved you, that you also love one another." This commandment summarizes all the others and expresses his entire will.

No. 2823: "He has made known to us the mystery of his will, according to his good pleasure that he set forth in Christ ... to gather up all things in him, things in heaven and things on earth. In Christ we have also obtained an inheritance, having been destined according to the purpose of him who accomplishes all things according to his counsel and will." We ask insistently for this loving plan to be fully realized on earth as it is already in heaven.

Give us this Day our Daily Bread

"It is written, 'Man shall not live by bread alone, but by every word that proceeds from the mouth of God'" (Mt 4:4).

After praying for those things that relate directly to the glory of God and His kingdom, we then ask God for those goods that are necessary to enable us to reach our temporal and eternal ends. This order was established by Christ Himself, in order that we may always seek first the glory of God in order to avoid being mindful only of ourselves: "... seek first his kingdom and his righteousness, and all these things shall be yours as well" (Mt 6:33).

It is necessary for Christians to have recourse to God for their temporal needs for since the Fall, mankind has been subject to the law of labor upon an earth cursed by God Himself: "cursed is the ground because of you; in toil you shall eat of it all the days of your life" (Gen. 3:17). This sentence still remains, an impediment to all man's efforts to secure prosperity. Yet, God still affords us His providence, and is ever willing to assist us in our needs: "For neither is there any god besides thee, whose care is for all men, to whom thou shouldst prove that thou hast not judged unjustly" (Wis. 12:13).

It is entirely lawful to pray for temporal necessities as "Good things and bad, life and death, poverty and wealth, come from the Lord." (Sir. 11:14). When asking for "our daily bread" we understand this to include all that is necessary for our sustenance, health, shelter and all our clothing needs. However, we should only ask for such goods as are in accord with our station of life. Furthermore, we are not to ask for even these in excessive quantities, instead we should be modest and temper our requests: "feed me with the food that is needful for me" (Prov. 30:8). Nor should we be haughty in our requests, but ask in a spirit of humility and dependence: "Let us fear the Lord our God, who gives the rain in its season, the autumn rain and the spring rain, and keeps for us the weeks appointed for the harvest" (Jer. 5:24).

Those who are satisfied in their temporal needs ought always to be thankful to God lest they commit the grave fault of ingratitude. Due to pride, we often forget to thank God for our riches and attribute our good fortune rather to our own efforts: "For all things come from thee, and of thy own have we given thee" (1 Chron. 29:14). Therefore, to humble ourselves, the prayer has "Give us" to remind us constantly that all things come from God.

Likewise, by using the word "daily" we show our utter dependence on God and the necessity to regularly turn to Him in our needs. The manna that fell from heaven with the dew each morning to feed the Jews for forty years in the wilderness lasted for only one day before it deteriorated. This was so to remind them of their daily dependence on God's providence (Num. 11:9). By praying daily we echo the spirit of the Psalmist, who declared: "The eyes of all look to thee, and thou givest them their food in due season" (Ps. 145:15). And in our prayers we should avoid excessive anxiety and fear, trusting in God's fatherly care: "... do not be anxious, saying, 'What shall we eat?' or 'What shall we drink?' or 'What shall we wear?' For the Gentiles seek all these things; and your heavenly Father knows that you need them all" (Mt 6:31-32).

Furthermore, we are commanded to pray that God may give "us" our daily bread so that we may be solicitous not only for our own needs, but for the needs of others. It is a duty pursuant upon all Christians to pray for the needs of others, including enemies. By doing this, we truly become "sons of your Father who is in heaven; for he makes his sun rise on the evil and on the good, and sends rain on the just and on the unjust" (Mt 5:45).

When praying for "our daily bread", the thoughts of the faithful should also be directed to asking God for our spiritual food, namely the word of God and the Blessed Eucharist. For both are described in Scripture as food, more vital than the food for our bodies: "It is written, 'Man shall not live by bread alone, but by every word that proceeds from the mouth of God'" (Mt 4:4); "the bread that I will give for the life of the world is my flesh" (Jn 6:51). By praying for and partaking of this food we seek to secure our eternal welfare for "he who eats this bread will live forever" (Jn 6:58).

The Fathers

Tertullian, *On Prayer* 6, 2 (inter AD 200-206)
"This petition 'Give us today our daily bread' we understand rather in a spiritual sense, for Christ is our bread because he is life and bread of life. 'I am the bread of life', he says, and, a little earlier, 'The bread is the word of the living God that has come down from heaven.' In addition, his body is a kind of bread: 'This is my body.' Consequently, in asking for daily bread, we are asking to live forever in Christ and never to be separated from his body."

St Cyprian of Carthage, *The Lord's Prayer* 18 (c. AD 251-252)
"As the prayer continues, we ask and say, 'Give us this day our daily bread' ... And we ask that this bread be given to us daily, so that we who are in Christ and daily receive the Eucharist as the food of salvation, may not, by falling into some more grievous sin and then in abstaining from communicating, be withheld from the heavenly Bread, and be separated from Christ's Body ... He Himself warns us, saying, 'Unless you eat the flesh of the Son of Man and drink His blood, you shall not have life in you.' Therefore do we ask that our Bread, which is Christ, be given to us daily, so that we who abide and live in Christ may not withdraw from His sanctification and from His Body."

St Cyril of Jerusalem, *Catechetical Lectures* 23, 15 (c. AD 350)
"Give us this day our supersubstantial bread. The bread which is of the common sort is not supersubstantial. But the Bread which is holy, that Bread is supersubstantial, as if to say, directed toward the substance of the soul. This Bread does not go into the belly, to be cast out into the privy. Rather, it is distributed through your whole system, for the benefit of body and soul."

St Augustine of Hippo, *Sermons* 57, 7 (inter AD 391-430)
"The Eucharist is our daily bread. The power belonging to this divine food makes it a bond of union. Its effect is then understood as unity, so that, gathered into his Body and made members of him, we may become what we receive ... This also is our daily bread: the readings you hear each

day in church and the hymns you hear and sing. All these are necessities for our pilgrimage."

The Roman Catechism (1566)

Pt. IV, Ch. XIII: ... the things necessary to human existence, or, at least, to its comfort, are almost innumerable; for by this knowledge of our wants and weaknesses, Christians will be compelled to have recourse to their heavenly Father, and humbly to ask of Him both earthly and spiritual blessings.

They will imitate the prodigal son, who, when he began to suffer want in a far distant country, and could find no one to give him even husks in his hunger, at length entering into himself, perceived that from the evils by which he was oppressed, he could expect relief from no one but from his father.

Catechism of the Catholic Church (1992)

No. 2828: *"Give us"*: The trust of children who look to their Father for everything is beautiful. "He makes his sun rise on the evil and on the good, and sends rain on the just and on the unjust." He gives to all the living "their food in due season." Jesus teaches us this petition, because it glorifies our Father by acknowledging how good he is, beyond all goodness.

No. 2830: *"Our bread"*: The Father who gives us life cannot but give us the nourishment life requires – all appropriate goods and blessings, both material and spiritual. In the Sermon on the Mount, Jesus insists on the filial trust that cooperates with our Father's providence. He is not inviting us to idleness, but wants to relieve us from nagging worry and preoccupation ...

And Forgive us our Trespasses

"... forgive, if you have anything against any one; so that your Father also who is in heaven may forgive you your trespasses" (Mk 11:25-26).

Nothing more illustrates the love that God has for all of mankind than His willingness to forgive sins. As a consequence of the Fall, we had all become "children of wrath" (Eph. 2:3), enemies of God and subjects of the kingdom of Satan. In a state of misery we deserved to stay, yet, despite our disobedience, God immediately promised a Messiah (Gen. 3:15) whose merits would deliver us from our sins and restore us to His friendship: "But God, who is rich in mercy, out of the great love with which he loved us, even when we were dead through our trespasses, made us alive together with Christ" (Eph. 2:4-5).

All are in need of forgiveness, for no one can claim to be free from sin: "If we say we have no sin, we deceive ourselves, and the truth is not in us" (1 Jn 1:8). In this petition we humble ourselves, admitting that we are all sinners and trespassers. When making this prayer, therefore, we should approach God seeking His mercy with sorrow and compunction for "equally hateful to God are the ungodly man and his ungodliness" (Wis. 14:9). However, compunction should always be coupled with confidence for "As a father pities his children, so the Lord pities those who fear him" (Ps. 103:13). We are encouraged to always live in hope of forgiveness, driving out all despair that could lead to more and greater sins: "I do not despair of my condition, for I have good hope of recovering from my illness" (2 Macc. 9:22).

Through this petition we may ask forgiveness for all our offenses, venial and mortal. With regard to mortal sins, however, the sacrament of Penance must be received or at least desired in order to procure forgiveness. Our Lord Jesus Christ, by instituting the sacrament of Penance after His resurrection (Jn 20:23), has endowed the Church with the very power He Himself possessed to forgive sins: "Take heart, son; your sins are forgiven" (Mt 9:2). This power continues to be exercised by the Church's bishops and priests spread today throughout the world, as a sign of the abundant mercy of God.

When confessing our sins we should readily admit all our offenses, not concealing or making excuses for any of them: "I acknowledged my sin to thee, and I did not hide my iniquity" (Ps. 32:5). Upon receiving forgiveness we should be exceedingly thankful: "Bless the Lord, O my soul, and forget not all his benefits, who forgives all your iniquity, who heals all your diseases" (Ps. 103:2-3). For we who were once offensive in God's sight have now been made clean: "though your sins are like scarlet, they shall be as white as snow; though they are red like crimson, they shall become like wool" (Is. 1:18).

The appendix to this petition states "as we forgive those who trespass against us." These words raise a condition vital for the forgiveness of our own sins. For if we are not prepared to forgive others, including enemies, neither will God forgive us: "Forgive your neighbor the wrong he has done, and then your sins will be pardoned when you pray" (Sir. 28:2); "forgive, if you have anything against any one; so that your Father also who is in heaven may forgive you your trespasses" (Mk 11:25-26). From this follows the beatitude "blessed are the merciful." To forgive those who offend us is perhaps the most difficult of all duties incumbent upon the Christian, yet Our Lord gave the ultimate example of such forgiveness when from the Cross He said, "Father, forgive them; for they know not what they do" (Lk 23:34). As God forgives us in the same measure we forgive others, our forgiveness of others should be generous: "... and if he sins against you seven times in the day, and turns to you seven times, and says, 'I repent', you must forgive him" (Lk 17:4); "I do not say to you seven times, but seventy times seven" (Mt 18:22).

The Fathers

St Cyprian of Carthage, *The Lord's Prayer* 23 (c. AD 251-252)
"God does not accept the sacrifice of a sower of disunion, but commands that he depart from the altar so that he may first be reconciled with his brother. For God can be appeased only by prayers that make peace. To God, the better offering is peace, brotherly concord, and a people made one in the unity of the Father, Son, and Holy Spirit."

St Cyprian of Carthage, *The Unity of the Catholic Church* **13 (inter AD 251-256)**
"Thus, also, when He gave the law of prayer, He added, saying, And when you stand praying, forgive, if you have anything against anyone; that your Father also who is in heaven may forgive you your trespasses. And He calls back from the altar one who comes to the sacrifice in strife, and bids him first agree with his brother, and then return with peace and offer his gift to God: for God had not respect unto Cain's offerings; for he could not have God at peace with him, who through envious discord had not peace with his brother."

St Cyril of Jerusalem, *Catechetical Lectures* **23, 16 (c. AD 350)**
"And forgive us our debts, as we also forgive our debtors. And we have many sins; for we offend both in word and in thought, and we do much that is worthy of condemnation. And, as John says, 'If we say that we have no sin, we lie.' We make a pact with God, entreating Him to forgive us our sins, just as we forgive our neighbors their debts. Considering then, what we receive and in return for what, let us neither delay nor postpone forgiving one another."

St Augustine of Hippo, *Against the Pelagians* **4, 10, 27 (AD 420)**
"Now let us see the third point which, in the Pelagians, is no less shocking to Christ's every member and to His whole body. They contend that in this life there are or have been righteous men having no sin at all. By this presumption they most clearly contradict the Lord's Prayer, in which all the members of Christ cry aloud with true heart these words to be said each day: 'Forgive us our debts.'"

St Augustine of Hippo, *The City of God* **Bk. 21, Ch. 27 (ante AD 427)**
"The daily prayer, which Jesus Himself taught and for which reason it is called the Lord's Prayer, certainly takes away daily sins, when we say daily: 'Forgive us our debts.'"

The Roman Catechism (1566)

Pt. IV, Ch. XIV: ... in this Petition, our Lord has taught how great is the goodness and bounty of God towards mankind; for if God were not ready and prepared to pardon penitents their sins, never would He have prescribed this formula of prayer: *Forgive us our trespasses.* Wherefore we ought to be firmly convinced, that since He commands us in this Petition to implore His paternal mercy, He will not fail to bestow it on us. For this Petition assuredly implies that God is so disposed towards us, as willingly to pardon those who are truly penitent.

Catechism of the Catholic Church (1992)

No. 2842: This "as" is not unique in Jesus' teaching; "You, therefore, must be perfect, *as* your heavenly Father is perfect"; "Be merciful, even *as* your Father is merciful"; "A new commandment I give to you, that you love one another, even *as* I have loved you, that you also love one another." It is impossible to keep the Lord's commandment by imitating the divine model from outside; there has to be a vital participation, coming from the depths of the heart, in the holiness and the mercy and the love of our God. Only the Spirit by whom we live can make "ours" the same mind that was in Christ Jesus. Then the unity of forgiveness becomes possible and we find ourselves "forgiving one another, *as* God in Christ forgave" us.

No. 2844: Christian prayer extends to the *forgiveness of enemies*, transfiguring the disciple by configuring him to his Master. Forgiveness is a high-point of Christian prayer; only hearts attuned to God's compassion can receive the gift of prayer. Forgiveness also bears witness that, in our world, love is stronger than sin. The martyrs of yesterday and today bear this witness to Jesus. Forgiveness is the fundamental condition of the reconciliation of the children of God with their Father and of men with one another.

And Lead us Not into Temptation

"God is faithful, and he will not let you be tempted beyond your strength" (1 Cor. 10:13).

In our weakened condition, we are constantly threatened with temptations coming from three sides: the world, the flesh and the Devil: "Has not man a hard service upon earth" (Job 7:1). It is therefore incumbent on all the faithful to be constantly on guard against temptation, invoking always the divine assistance in times of danger. Hence, Our Lord's admonition in this prayer and elsewhere to "Pray that you may not enter into temptation" (Mt 26:41).

By the spirit of the world, we mean that spirit which seeks only pleasure, wealth, popularity and power, while ignoring heaven and all that is necessary to acquire it. Those infected with this spirit despise the Christian life and those who follow it: "If you were of the world, the world would love its own; but because you are not of the world, but I chose you out of the world, therefore the world hates you" (Jn 15:19). We should set our sights on conforming our lives to Christ, placing our first love in heavenly things: "Do not be conformed to this world" (Rom. 12:2); "Do not love the world or the things in the world" (1 Jn 2:15). If we are not relentless in struggling against the world we are destined to be overwhelmed by it: "And as for what fell among the thorns, they are those who hear, but as they go on their way they are choked by the cares and riches and pleasures of life, and their fruit does not mature" (Lk 8:14).

Temptations of the flesh for many are the most troubling because of our in-born weakness due to original sin. Our desires are no longer subject to reason but instead war against it: "For the desires of the flesh are against the Spirit, and the desires of the Spirit are against the flesh" (Gal. 5:17). Without God's grace we would often be overwhelmed by lust for "the spirit indeed is willing, but the flesh is weak" (Mk 14:38). No one is free from the concupiscence of the flesh, not even some of the greatest saints: "And to keep me from being too elated by the abundance of revelations, a thorn was given me in the flesh, a messenger of Satan, to harass me, to keep me from being too elated" (2 Cor. 12:7).

The most malignant source of all our temptations is Satan who "prowls around like a roaring lion, seeking some one to devour" (1 Pet. 5:8); "For we are not contending against flesh and blood, but against the principalities, against the powers, against the world rulers of this present darkness, against the spiritual hosts of wickedness in the heavenly places" (Eph. 6:12). Satan constantly try to assail us from without, insinuating evil purposes and depraved desires into our minds. At worst, the demons may possess a body in order to lead a person into sin and spiritual destruction: "Then he goes and brings with him seven other spirits more evil than himself, and they enter and dwell there" (Mt 12:45).

In the face of such enemies we may be tempted to despair. However, "You shall not fear them; for it is the Lord your God who fights for you" (Deut. 3:22). All temptation can be overcome with God's help: "God is faithful, and he will not let you be tempted beyond your strength" (1 Cor. 10:13). Also, in Christ Himself we have a compassionate advocate who while on earth was "tempted as we are, yet without sin" (Heb. 4:15).

No one is led into temptation by God for "he himself tempts no one" (Js. 1:13). It may be the case, though, that God allows temptation for His greater glory and to prove our love for Him: "And because thou wast acceptable to God, it was necessary that temptation should prove thee" (Tob. 12:13). Temptation faithfully repulsed, also redounds to our honor and glory: "so that the genuineness of your faith, more precious than gold which though perishable is tested by fire, may redound to praise and glory and honor at the revelation of Jesus Christ" (1 Pet. 1:7).

When praying to be delivered from temptation we should be animated by a spirit of humility, distrusting ourselves and placing our confidence in God: "be of good cheer; I have conquered the world!" (Jn 16:33). Our prayer may be directed against one particular temptation or against all temptations in general: "Lord, Father and God of my life, do not give me haughty eyes, and remove from me evil desire. Let neither gluttony nor lust overcome me, and do not surrender me to a shameless soul" (Sir. 23:5-6). Victory over temptation belongs to God: "Not to us, O Lord, not to us; but to thy name give glory" (Ps. 115:1); and the reward for final victory is exceedingly great: "He who conquers, I will grant him to sit with me on my throne" (Rev. 3:21).

The Fathers

Tertullian, *On Prayer* 8 (inter AD 200-206)
"'Lead us not into temptation': in other words, do not let us be led astray by the Tempter. Let us not even think that the Lord appears to be the one who tempts us – as if he were not aware of the faith of an individual or, even, were bent on disturbing it! That kind of weakness and malice belongs to the devil. Even in the case of Abraham, God commanded the sacrifice of his son not to tempt his faith, but to prove it. In Abraham, God would set an example of that precept by which he was to teach, in time, that no one should love even his nearest and dearest more than God. Christ, himself, was tempted by the devil and unmasked for us that subtle master of temptation. He emphasizes this petition at a later time when he says, 'Pray that you enter not into temptation.' Still, they were tempted and deserted their Lord, falling asleep rather than persevering in prayer. Thus, the last phrase of this petition balances the first and points to its meaning: 'Lead us not into temptation'; 'but deliver us from evil'."

Origen, *On Prayer* 29 (post AD 231)
"There is a certain usefulness to temptation. No one but God knows what our soul has received from him, not even we ourselves. But temptation reveals it in order to teach us to know ourselves, and in this way we discover our evil inclinations and are obliged to give thanks for the goods that temptation has revealed to us."

St Cyril of Jerusalem, *Catechetical Lectures* 23, 17 (c. AD 350)
"And lead us not, O Lord, into temptation. That we should pray not to be tempted at all – is this what the Lord teaches? How then is it written elsewhere, 'A man untempted is a reprobate'? And again, 'Count it all joy, my brethren, when you fall into various temptations.' But wait –does not 'being led into temptation' really mean 'being submerged by temptation'? For temptation is like a winter torrent, something difficult through which to pass."

St Gregory of Nyssa, *The Lord's Prayer* Sermon 5 (inter AD 371-395)
"'Lead us not into temptation, but deliver us from evil.' My friends, what do these words mean? It seems that the Lord gives many different names

to the evil one, each suited to the difference among evil actions. So, he is devil, Beelzebub, Mammon, prince of this world, murderer of humankind, the evil one, the father of lies, and other similar names. Perhaps, in this instance, one of the names attributed to him is 'temptation.'"

The Roman Catechism (1566)

Pt. IV, Ch. XV: We should, therefore, implore the divine assistance, in general, against all temptations, and especially when assailed by any particular temptation. This we find to have been the conduct of David, under almost every species of temptation. Against lying he prays in these words: *Take not thou the word of truth utterly out of my mouth*; against covetousness: *Incline my heart unto thy testimonies, and not to covetousness*; and against the vanities of this life and the allurements of concupiscence, he prays thus: *Turn away my eyes, that they may not behold vanity.*

We pray, therefore, that we yield not to evil desires, and be not wearied in enduring temptation; that we *deviate not from the way of the Lord*; that in adversity, as in prosperity, we preserve equanimity and fortitude; and that God may never deprive us of His protection. Finally, we pray that God may *crush Satan beneath our feet.*

Catechism of the Catholic Church (1992)

No. 2846: This petition goes to the root of the preceding one, for our sins result from our consenting to temptation; we therefore ask our Father not to "lead" us into temptation. It is difficult to translate the Greek verb used by a single English word: the Greek means both "do not allow us to enter into temptation" and "do not let us yield to temptation." "God cannot be tempted by evil and he himself tempts no one"; on the contrary, he wants to set us free from evil. We ask him not to allow us to take the way that leads to sin. We are engaged in the battle "between flesh and spirit"; this petition implores the Spirit of discernment and strength.

But Deliver us from Evil. Amen.

"Blessed be the God and Father of our Lord Jesus Christ, the Father of mercies and God of all comfort, who comforts us in all our affliction" (2 Cor. 1:3-4).

Since the Fall, man has constantly been exposed to numerous evils and calamities, emanating from the world, the flesh and the Devil. We are so afflicted that not only did Christ command us to pray to be delivered from evil, but He Himself prayed to God for our deliverance (Jn 17:15). Indeed, no day passes without trial, as is implied in Our Lord's admonition to "take up (our) cross daily and follow me" (Lk 9:23). Furthermore, it is the special lot of the just to suffer persecution in this world, for as St Paul says "all who desire to live a godly life in Christ Jesus will be persecuted" (2 Tim. 3:12).

Tribulations are allowed to afflict us through the permissive will of God. They are permitted, firstly, to test us: "If thou triest my heart, if thou visitest me by night, if thou testest me, thou wilt find no wickedness in me; my mouth does not transgress" (Ps. 17:3); to chastise us: "My son, do not despise the Lord's discipline or be weary of his reproof for the Lord reproves him whom he loves" (Prov. 3:11-12); and to save us: "Come, let us return to the Lord for he has torn, that he may heal us; he has stricken, and he will bind us up" (Hos. 6:1).

When visited by tribulation, the chief hope of the Christian is confidence in God as the comforter of the afflicted: "Blessed be the God and Father of our Lord Jesus Christ, the Father of mercies and God of all comfort, who comforts us in all our affliction" (2 Cor. 1:3-4). Numerous are the examples in Scripture which testify to God's merciful goodness in times of trial, the leading being the story of Job. With such a history of mercy, how could Christians other than have confidence in God: "When I think of thy ordinances from of old, I take comfort, O Lord" (Ps. 119:52). Christians should also remember that, for our sake, God often shortens the trial and that "after the storm you make a calm" (Tob. 3:22).

We pray to be delivered from evils such as war, famine, disease, untimely death, etc. In addition, Catholics should pray to be delivered from the spirit of the world and its lure of false riches, honors and pleasures. All things contrary to our spiritual interests are evils to be prayed against. This is so particularly with respect to the enemy of our salvation who "prowls around like a roaring lion, seeking some one to devour" (1 Pet. 5:8). In some cases, God may permit the Devil to tempt us for our spiritual advantage, and to show forth His power: "And to keep me from being too elated by the abundance of revelations, a thorn was given me in the flesh, a messenger of Satan, to harass me ... Three times I besought the Lord about this, that it should leave me; but he said to me, 'My grace is sufficient for you, for my power is made perfect in weakness'" (2 Cor. 12:7-9).

In the midst of tribulations Catholics should show patience, praying continuously in the spirit of submission to God's will, avoiding all murmuring and discontent: "But they that did not receive the trials with the fear of the Lord, but uttered their impatience and the reproach of their murmuring against the Lord, were destroyed by the destroyer" (Jud. 8:24-25). It should always be kept in mind that it is only "through many tribulations we must enter the kingdom of God" (Acts 14:22) and that "momentary affliction is preparing for us an eternal weight of glory beyond all comparison" (2 Cor. 4:17). Finally, in the spirit of the Apostles we should actually rejoice in tribulation, particularly when we are called upon to suffer for the Faith: "Then they left the presence of the council, rejoicing that they were counted worthy to suffer dishonor for the name" (Acts 5:41).

Amen

The great prayer of Our Lord Jesus Christ is terminated by the word "Amen." Many are the explanations that can be attached to the meaning of this word in this context. It may signify that the prayer has been heard, or is the final earnest call upon God to speedily grant the petitions just asked for.

The Fathers

Origen, *On Prayer* 30 (post AD 231)
"Now, God 'delivers us from evil,' not when the Adversary refrains from attacking us with whatever tricks he has, but rather when we courageously face whatever comes to us and, thus, conquer him. This is the interpretation we give to the words, 'Many are the afflictions of the just, but out of them all God delivers them.' God delivers us from afflictions, not when afflictions no longer weigh upon us--for Paul says that we are at no time without affliction: 'In all things we are afflicted.' Rather, we are delivered when, though afflicted, with God's help, 'we are not distressed.' According to a Hebrew idiom, to be 'afflicted' means to endure a critical situation that arises against a person's will. To be 'distressed,' on the contrary, refers to a state which does arise from the will to the extent that an individual is overcome by affliction and yields to it. Thus, Paul is right in saying, 'In all things we are afflicted, but are not distressed.'"

St Cyprian of Carthage, *The Lord's Prayer* 27 (c. AD 251-252)
"At the very end, we pray, 'But deliver us from evil.' By this, we include all the trials which the enemy seeks to inflict on us in this world. We can find strong and faithful protection against such evil, if God delivers us and if he grants us his aid, as we pray and beseech him. When we say, 'Deliver us from evil', there is nothing left to ask for. Once we have sought and obtained God's protection against evil, we are safe and secure against all the works of the devil and the evils of the world. Who of us can be afraid of the world, if God is for us as our protector?"

St Cyril of Jerusalem, *Catechetical Lectures* 23, 18 (c. AD 350)
"But deliver us from evil. If 'lead us not into temptation' meant not being tempted at all, He would not have said, 'But deliver us from evil.' Evil signifies the demon adversary, from whom we pray to be delivered. Then, after the prayer has been completed, you say, 'Amen.' Through this Amen, which signifies So be it, you set your seal upon the petitions of this divinely-taught prayer."

St Ambrose of Milan, *The Sacraments* 5, 4, 30 (AD 390-391)
"The Lord who has taken away your sin and pardoned your faults also protects you and keeps you from the wiles of your adversary the devil, so that the enemy, who is accustomed to leading into sin, may not surprise you. One who entrusts himself to God does not dread the devil. 'If God is for us, who is against us?'"

The Roman Catechism (1566)

Pt. IV, Ch. XVI: The full meaning of this Petition, therefore, is, that having been freed from sin and from the danger of temptation, we may be delivered from internal and external evils; that we may be protected from floods, fire and lightning; that the fruits of the earth be not destroyed by hail; that we be not visited by famine, sedition or war. We ask that God may banish disease, pestilence and disaster from us; that He may keep us from slavery, imprisonment, exile, betrayals, treachery, and from all other evils which fill mankind with terror and misery. Finally, we pray that God would remove all occasions of sin and iniquity.

Catechism of the Catholic Church (1992)

No. 2851: In this petition, evil is not an abstraction, but refers to a person, Satan, the Evil One, the angel who opposes God. The devil (*diabolos*) is the one who "throws himself across" God's plan and his work of salvation accomplished by Christ.

No. 2854: When we ask to be delivered from the Evil One, we pray as well to be freed from all evils, present, past, and future, of which he is the author or instigator. In this final petition, the Church brings before the Father all the distress of the world. Along with deliverance from the evils that overwhelm humanity, she implores the precious gift of peace and the grace of perseverance in expectation of Christ's return. By praying in this way, she anticipates in humility of faith the gathering together of everyone and everything in him who has "the keys of death and Hades", who "is and who was and who is to come, the Almighty."

Appendices

Appendix A

COUNCIL OF TRENT
DECREE ON JUSTIFICATION
13 January, 1547

Chapter 11
On Keeping the Commandments, and on the Necessity and Possibility Thereof.

But no one, however much justified, should think himself exempt from the observance of the commandments; no one should use that rash saying, one prohibited by the Fathers under an anathema, that the observance of the commandments of God is impossible for one who is justified. "For God does not command impossibilities, but, by commanding, both admonishes you to do what you can, and to pray for what you can not"[1], and aids you that you may be able; "whose commandments are not heavy" (1 Jn 5:3), whose "yoke is sweet, and burden light" (Mt 11:30). For they who are the sons of God love Christ; but they who love Him keep His commandments (Jn 14:23), as He Himself testifies; which indeed with divine help they can do. For though during this mortal life, men, however holy and just, at times fall into at least light and daily sins, which are also called venial, they do not on that account cease to be just. For that cry of the just, "forgive us our trespasses", (Mt 6:12) is both humble and true. For this cause, the just themselves ought to feel themselves more obliged to walk in the way of justice, in that, being already "freed from sin, and made servants of God" (Rom. 6:22), they are able, "living soberly, justly, and godly" (Tit. 2:12), to proceed onwards through Jesus Christ, by Whom they have had access unto this grace (Rom. 5:2). For God does not forsake those who have been once justified by His grace, unless He be first forsaken by them.

---

[1] St Augustine, *On Nature and Grace* 43, 50.

Wherefore, no one ought to flatter himself with faith alone, thinking that by faith alone he is made an heir, and will obtain the inheritance, even though he not "suffer with Christ, that he may also be glorified with Him" (Rom. 8:17). For even Christ Himself, as the Apostle says, "whereas He was the Son of God, learned obedience by the things which He suffered, and, being consummated, He became to all who obey Him the cause of eternal salvation" (Heb. 5:8 f.). For which reason, the same Apostle admonishes the justified, saying: "Do you not know that they who run in the race all run indeed, but one receives the prize? So run that you may obtain. I therefore so run, not as at an uncertainty; I so fight, not as one beating the air, but I chastize my body, and bring it into subjection; lest perhaps when I have preached to others, I myself should become a castaway" (1 Cor. 9:24, 26-27). So also the prince of the Apostles, Peter: "Labor the more that by good works you may make sure your calling and election. For doing these things, you shall not sin at any time" (2 Pet.1:10). From which it is plain, that they are opposed to the orthodox doctrine of religion who assert that the just man sins at least venially in every good work, or (what is more intolerable) that he merits eternal punishments; as also those who state that the just sin in all their works, if in order to arouse their laziness and to encourage themselves to run the race, they, in addition to this, that above all God may be glorified, have in view also the eternal reward; since it is written: "I have inclined my heart to keep all your statutes for the reward" (Ps. 118:112); and concerning Moses the Apostle says that "he looked unto the reward" (Heb. 11:26).

Canon 17

If anyone says that the grace of justification is attained only by those who are predestined unto life, but that all others who are called are called indeed, but do not receive grace, as if by divine power they are predestined unto evil: let him be anathema.

Canon 18

If anyone says that the commandments of God are impossible to keep, even for one who is justified and constituted in grace: let him be anathema.

Canon 19
If anyone says that nothing besides faith is commanded in the Gospel; that other things are indifferent, neither commanded nor prohibited, but free; or that the Ten Commandments in no way pertain to Christians: let him be anathema.

Canon 20
If anyone says that a man who is justified and ever so perfect is not bound to observe the Commandments of God and of the Church, but only to believe; as if indeed the Gospel were a bare and absolute promise of eternal life, without the condition of observance of the Commandments: let him be anathema.

Appendix B

MAGISTERIAL DECREES AND DOCUMENTS
ON THE
SACRAMENTS IN GENERAL

POPE INNOCENT III
PROFESSION OF FAITH PRESCRIBED FOR THE WALDENSIANS
AD 1208

Furthermore, we do not reject the sacraments which are conferred in the Church, in co-operation with the inestimable and invisible power of the Holy Spirit, even though these sacraments be administered by a sinful priest, as long as he is recognized by the Church. And we do not disparage ecclesiastical duties and blessings performed by such a one; but we accept them with benevolence, as we would those performed by the most just man. For the evil life of a bishop or a priest has no harmful effect on either the baptism of an infant or the consecration of the Eucharist or other ecclesiastical duties performed for the faithful.

THE SECOND GENERAL COUNCIL OF LYONS
PROFESSION OF FAITH OF MICHAEL PALAEOLOGUS
AD 1274

The same Holy Roman Church also holds and teaches that there are seven sacraments of the Church: one is baptism, which has been mentioned above; another is the sacrament of confirmation which bishops confer by the laying on of hands while they anoint the reborn; then penance, the Eucharist, the sacrament of order, matrimony and extreme unction which, according to the doctrine of the Blessed James, is administered to the sick. The same Roman Church performs the sacrament of the Eucharist with unleavened bread; she holds and teaches that in this sacrament the bread is truly transubstantiated into the body of our Lord Jesus Christ, and the wine into His blood. As regards matrimony, she holds that neither is a man allowed to have several wives at the same time nor a woman several husbands. But, when a legitimate marriage is dissolved by the death of one of the spouses, she declares that a second and afterwards a third wedding are successively licit, if no other canonical impediment goes against it for any reason.

THE GENERAL COUNCIL OF CONSTANCE
CONDEMNATION OF ERRORS OF WYCLIFFE AND HUSS
AD 1415

Error condemned:
If a bishop or priest is in mortal sin, he does not ordain, he does not consecrate, he does not perform (the Eucharist), he does not baptize.

POPE MARTIN V
BULL *INTER CUNCTAS*
AD 1418

Proposition addressed to the followers of Wycliffe and Huss:
... a bad priest who uses the correct matter and form and has the intention of doing what the Church does, truly performs (the Eucharist), truly absolves, truly baptizes, truly confers the other sacraments.

THE GENERAL COUNCIL OF FLORENCE
DECREE FOR THE ARMENIANS
AD 1439

We here set out the true doctrine of the sacraments of the Church in a brief formula which will facilitate the instruction of the Armenians, both now and in the future. There are seven sacraments of the New Law, namely, baptism, confirmation, the Eucharist, penance, extreme unction, Order and matrimony; and they differ greatly from the sacraments of the Old Law. For these did not cause grace but were only a figure of the grace that was to be given through the passion of Christ; but our sacraments both contain grace and confer it on those who receive them worthily.

The first five of these are ordained to the interior spiritual perfection of the person himself; the last two are ordained to the government and the increase of the whole Church. For by baptism we are spiritually reborn and by confirmation we grow in grace and are strengthened in the faith; being reborn and strengthened, we are nourished with the divine food of the Eucharist. If by sin we become sick in soul, we are healed spiritually by penance; by extreme unction, we are also healed in spirit, and in body in so far as it is good for the soul. Through Order the Church is governed and receives spiritual growth; through matrimony she receives bodily growth.

All these sacraments are constituted by three elements: by things as the matter, by words as the form, and by the person of the minister conferring the sacrament with the intention of doing what the Church does. And if any one of these three is lacking, the sacrament is not effected.

Among these sacraments there are three, baptism, confirmation and Order, which imprint on the soul an indelible character, that is a certain spiritual sign distinguishing (the recipient) from others. Hence, these are not repeated for the same person. The other four, however, do not imprint a character and may be repeated.

POPE LEO X
BULL *EXSURGE DOMINE*
AD 1520

Error of Luther condemned:
It is a heretical, though widespread, opinion that the sacraments of the New Law give justifying grace to those who do not place an obstacle in the way.

THE GENERAL COUNCIL OF TRENT
DECREE ON THE SACRAMENTS
AD 1547

Foreword
In order to bring to completion the salutary doctrine of justification promulgated with the unanimous consent of the Fathers in the session

immediately preceding, it seemed fitting to deal with the holy sacraments of the Church. For all true justification either begins through the sacraments, or, once begun, increases through them, or when lost, is regained through them. Therefore, in order to do away with errors and to root out heresies which in this our age are directed against the holy sacraments – partly inspired by heresies already condemned in the past by our Fathers and partly newly devised – and which are doing great harm to the purity of the Catholic Church and to the salvation of souls, the most holy, ecumenical and general Council of Trent, lawfully assembled in the Holy Spirit under the presidency of the same legates of the apostolic See, adhering to the teaching of the Holy Scriptures, to the apostolic traditions and to the consensus of the Fathers and of the other Councils, has thought that the present canons should be drawn up and decreed. The canons which remain for the completion of the work begun, the Council will, with the help of the Holy Spirit, publish hereafter.

Canons on the Sacraments in General

1. If anyone says that the sacraments of the New Law were not all instituted by Jesus Christ our Lord; or that there are more or fewer than seven, that is: baptism, confirmation, the Eucharist, penance, extreme unction, Order and matrimony; or that any one of these is not truly and properly a sacrament, let him be anathema.

2. If anyone says that these same sacraments of the New Law do not differ from the sacraments of the Old Law, except that the ceremonies and external rites are different, let him be anathema.

3. If anyone says that these sacraments are so equal to one another that no one is for any reason of any greater worth than another, let him be anathema.

4. If anyone says that the sacraments of the New Law are not necessary for salvation, but that they are superfluous; and that without the sacraments or the desire of them men obtain from God the grace of justification through faith alone, although it is true that not all the sacraments are necessary for each person, let him be anathema.

5. If anyone says that these sacraments are instituted only for the sake of nourishing faith, let him be anathema.

6. If anyone says that the sacraments of the New Law do not

contain the grace which they signify or that they do not confer that grace on those who place no obstacle in the way, as if they were only external signs of the grace or justice received through faith and a kind of marks of the Christian profession by which among men the faithful are distinguished from unbelievers, let him be anathema.

7. If anyone says that, as far as God's part is concerned, grace is not given through these sacraments always and to all, even if they receive them rightly, but only sometimes and to some, let him be anathema.

8. If anyone says that through the sacraments of the New Law grace is not conferred by the performance of the rite itself (*ex opere operato*) but that faith alone in the divine promise is sufficient to obtain grace, let him be anathema.

9. If anyone says that in three sacraments, namely, baptism, confirmation and Order, a character is not imprinted on the soul, that is, a kind of indelible spiritual sign by reason of which these sacraments cannot be repeated, let him be anathema.

10. If anyone says that all Christians have the power (to preach) the word and to administer all the sacraments, let him be anathema.

11. If anyone says that the intention, at least of doing what the Church does, is not required in the ministers when they are performing and conferring the sacraments, let him be anathema.

12. If anyone says that a minister in the state of mortal sin, though he observes all the essentials that belong to the performing and conferring of the sacrament, does not perform or confer the sacrament, let him be anathema.

13. If anyone says that the accepted and approved rites of the Catholic Church which are customarily used in the solemn administration of the sacraments may be despised or omitted without sin by the ministers as they please, or that they may be changed to other new rites by any pastor in the Church, let him be anathema.

THE GENERAL COUNCIL OF TRENT
DOCTRINE ON COMMUNION UNDER BOTH SPECIES AND ON COMMUNION OF LITTLE CHILDREN
AD 1562

Chapter 2: The Power of the Church concerning the Dispensation of

the Sacrament of the Eucharist.

(The Holy Council) furthermore declares that in the dispensation of the sacraments, provided their substance is preserved, the Church has always had the power to determine or change, according to circumstances, times and places, what she judges more expedient for the benefit of the recipients or for the veneration of the sacraments. It seems that the Apostle referred to this power rather clearly when he said: "This is how one should regard us, as servants of Christ and stewards of the mysteries of God" (1 Cor. 4:1). It is sufficiently clear that he himself used this power not only in many other instances but also with regard to this very sacrament, when he laid down certain regulations for its use and said: "About the other things I will give directions when I come" (1 Cor. 11:34). Therefore ... holy Mother Church, conscious of her authority in the administration of the sacraments ...
(There follows the approval of Communion under one kind).

POPE ALEXANDER VIII
DECREE OF THE HOLY OFFICE
AD 1690

Error of the Jansenists condemned:

Baptism is valid, when conferred by a minister who observes all the external rites and the form of baptizing, but interiorly within his heart resolves: I do not intend what the Church does.

POPE ST PIUS X
DECREE *LAMENTABILI* OF THE HOLY OFFICE
AD 1907

Modernist propositions condemned:

39. The opinions on the origin of the sacraments with which the Tridentine Fathers were imbued and which undoubtedly influenced their dogmatic canons are far removed from those which are now rightly held by research historians of Christianity.

40. The sacraments owe their origin to the fact that the apostles and their successors interpreted some idea and intention of Christ under the influence and pressure of circumstances and events.

41. The purpose of the sacraments is only to recall to the mind of man the ever beneficent presence of the Creator.

POPE ST PIUS X
ENCYCLICAL LETTER *PASCENDI*
AD 1907

On the question of worship, little would have to be said were it not for the fact that the sacraments come under this heading; and here the Modernists fall into the gravest errors. They attempt to show that worship results from a twofold impulse or necessity; for, as we have seen, everything in their system is explained by inner impulses or necessities. The first impulse is to attribute some sensible element to religion; the second impulse is to make it known, and this could not be done without some sensible form and sanctifying actions which we call sacraments. For the Modernists, the sacraments are mere symbols or signs, though not altogether without power. To explain the nature of this power, they compare it to the power of certain phrases which in common parlance "have caught on," inasmuch as they have acquired the power of propagating mighty ideas capable of deeply striking men's minds. What these phrases are to ideas, the sacraments are to the religious sense – that, and nothing more. Now, surely, the Modernists would speak more plainly, were they to affirm that the sacraments were instituted solely to foster faith. But this the Council of Trent has condemned: "If anyone says that these sacraments were instituted only for the sake of nourishing faith, let him be anathema."

POPE PIUS XII
ENCYCLICAL LETTER *MYSTICI CORPORIS*
AD 1943

The human body ... has its own means for fostering the life, health and growth of itself and each of its members. And the Savior of the human race in His infinite goodness has in like manner admirably equipped His mystical Body by endowing it with the sacraments, making available for its members a progressive series of graces to sustain them from the cradle to their last breath, and abundantly providing also for the social needs of the whole Body. By baptism those who have been born to this mortal life are regenerated from the death of sin and made members of the Church, and also invested with a spiritual character which makes them able and fit to receive the other sacraments. The chrism of confirmation gives believers new strength so that they may strenuously guard and defend Mother Church and the faith which they have received from her. The sacrament of penance offers a saving remedy to members of the Church who have fallen into sin, and this not only for the sake of their own salvation but also in order that their fellow-members may be saved from the danger of contagion, and receive instead an example and incentive to virtue. Nor is this all: in the Holy Eucharist the faithful are nourished and fortified at a common banquet, and by an ineffable and divine bond united with one another and with the divine Head of the whole Body. And when at last they are mortally ill, loving Mother Church is at their side with the sacrament of extreme unction, and although, God so willing, she may not always thereby restore health of the body, she nevertheless applies a supernatural balm to the wounded soul, thus providing new citizens for heaven and new heavenly intercessors for herself, who will enjoy the divine goodness for all eternity.

For the social needs of the Church Christ has also provided in a particular way by two other sacraments which He instituted. The sacrament of matrimony, in which the partners become the ministers of grace to each other, ensures the regular numerical increase of the Christian community, and, what is more important, the proper and religious education of the offspring, the lack of which would constitute a grave menace to the mystical Body. And holy Order, finally, consecrates to the perpetual service of God those who are destined to offer the eucharistic victim, to nourish the flock of the faithful with the bread of angels and with the food of doctrine, to guide them by the divine commandments and counsels, and to fortify them by their other supernatural functions.

Christ is the author and efficient cause of holiness; for there can be no salutary act which does not proceed from Him as from its supernatural source: "Apart from Me you can do nothing," He said (Jn

15:5) ... His inexhaustible fullness is the fount of grace and glory ... And when the Church administers the sacraments with external rites, it is He who produces their effect in the soul. He it is, too, who feeds the redeemed with His own flesh and blood ...

... In the first place, in virtue of the juridical mission by which the divine Redeemer sent forth His apostles into the world as He Himself had been sent by the Father (cf. Jn 17:18; 20:21), it is indeed He who baptizes through the Church, He who teaches, governs, absolves, binds, offers and makes sacrifice.

POPE PIUS XII
ENCYCLICAL LETTER *MEDIATOR DEI*
AD 1947

In the whole conduct of the liturgy the Church has her divine founder present with her. Christ is present in the august sacrifice of the altar, both in the person of His minister and especially under the eucharistic species; He is present in the sacraments by His power which He infuses into them as instruments of sanctification; He is present, finally, in the prayer and praise which are offered to God, in accordance with His promise: "Where two or three are gathered in my name, there am I in the midst of them" (Mt. 18:20).

It is certainly true that the sacraments and the Mass possess an intrinsic efficacy, because they are actions of Christ Himself transmitting and distributing the grace of the divine Head to the members of the mystical Body. But to have their proper effect they require our souls also to be in the right dispositions. This is why St Paul warns us in regard to the Eucharist: "Let a man examine himself, and so eat of the bread and drink of the cup" (1 Cor. 11:28) ... For it must be borne in mind that the members of this Body are living members, endowed with intellect and will; therefore they must deliberately set their lips to this source of grace, absorb and assimilate this food of life, and uproot from themselves anything that may obscure its efficacy. So the work of our redemption, though in itself something independent of our will, really calls for an interior effort from our souls if we are to attain eternal salvation.

... The liturgical year, animated throughout by the devotion of the Church, is no cold and lifeless representation of past events, no mere historical record. It is Christ Himself, living on in His Church, and still pursuing that path of boundless mercy which, going about doing good (cf. Acts 10:38), He began to tread during His life on earth. This He did in order that the souls of men might come into contact with His mysteries and, so to speak, live by them. And these mysteries are still now constantly present and active, not in the vague and nebulous way which recent authors describe, but as Catholic doctrine teaches us. The Doctors of the Church tell us that the mysteries of Christ's life are at the same time most excellent models of virtue for us to imitate and also sources of divine grace for us by reason of the merits and intercession of the Redeemer. They live on in their effect in us, since each of them is, according to its nature and in its own way, the cause of our salvation.

THE SECOND VATICAN GENERAL COUNCIL
CONSTITUTION *SACROSANCTUM CONCILIUM*
AD 1963

7. To accomplish so great a work, Christ is always present to His Church, especially in her liturgical celebrations. He is present in the sacrifice of the Mass, not only in the person of His minister, "the same now offering through the ministry of priests, who then offered Himself on the cross", but especially under the eucharistic species. By His power He is present in the sacraments, so that when a man baptizes it is really Christ Himself who baptizes. He is present in His word, since it is He Himself who speaks when the Holy Scriptures are read in the Church. He is present, lastly, when the Church prays and sings, for He promised: "Where two or three are gathered in my name, there am I in the midst of them."

8. Christ indeed always associates the Church with Himself in this great work wherein God is perfectly glorified and men are sanctified. The Church is His beloved Bride who calls to her Lord and through Him offers worship to the eternal Father. Rightly, then, the liturgy is considered as an exercise of the priestly office of Jesus Christ. In the liturgy the sanctification of man is signified by signs perceptible to the senses, and is effected in a way which corresponds with each of these signs; in the liturgy the whole public worship is performed by the mystical Body of Jesus Christ, that is, by the Head and His members ...

9. The purpose of the sacraments is to sanctify men, to build up

the Body of Christ, and, finally, to give worship to God; because they are signs, they also instruct. They not only presuppose faith, but by words and objects they also nourish, strengthen and express it; that is why they are called "sacraments of faith." They do indeed impart grace, but, in addition, the very act of celebrating them most effectively disposes the faithful to receive this grace in a fruitful manner, to worship God duly, and to practise charity.

It is therefore of the highest importance that the faithful should easily understand the sacramental signs, and should frequent with great eagerness those sacraments which were instituted to nourish the Christian life.

POPE PAUL VI
APOSTOLIC EXHORTATION *EVANGELII NUNTIANDI*
AD 1975

47. Evangelization exercises its full capacity when it achieves the most intimate relationship, or better still a permanent and unbroken inter-communication, between the Word and the Sacraments. In a certain sense it is a mistake to build a contrast between evangelization and sacramentalization, as is sometimes done. It is indeed true that a certain way of administering the Sacraments, without the solid support of catechesis regarding these same Sacraments and a global catechesis, could end up by depriving them of their effectiveness to a great extent. The role of evangelization is precisely to educate people in the faith in such a way as to lead each individual Christian to live the Sacraments as true Sacraments of faith – and not to receive them passively or to undergo them.

Appendix C

PRAYERS

"Lord, teach us to pray ..." (Lk 11:1)

The Sign of the Cross

In the name of the Father, and of the Son, and of the Holy Spirit. Amen.

The Apostles' Creed

I believe in God, the Father Almighty, Creator of heaven and earth; and in Jesus Christ, His only Son, Our Lord; Who was conceived by the Holy Spirit, born of the Virgin Mary, suffered under Pontius Pilate, was crucified, died, and was buried. He descended into hell; the third day He rose again from the dead; He ascended into heaven, sitteth at the right hand of God, the Father Almighty; from thence He shall come to judge the living and the dead. I believe in the Holy Spirit, the Holy Catholic Church, the communion of saints, the forgiveness of sins, the resurrection of the body, and life everlasting. Amen.

The Lord's Prayer

Our Father Who art in heaven, hallowed be Thy name; Thy kingdom come, Thy will be done on earth as it is in heaven. Give us this day our daily bread; and forgive us our trespasses, as we forgive those who trespass against us; and lead us not into temptation, but deliver us from evil. Amen.

The Hail Mary

Hail Mary, full of grace; the Lord is with thee; blessed art thou among women, and blessed is the fruit of thy womb, Jesus. Holy Mary, Mother of God, pray for us sinners, now and at the hour of our death. Amen.

The Glory Be

Glory be to the Father, and to the Son, and to the Holy Spirit. As it was in the beginning, is now and ever shall be, world without end. Amen.

O My Jesus

O my Jesus, forgive us our sins, save us from the fires of hell; lead all souls to heaven, especially those in most need of Thy mercy.

The Morning Offering

O Jesus, through the most pure Heart of Mary, I offer Thee the prayers, works, joys and sufferings of this day for all the intentions of Thy divine Heart.

Grace Before Meals

Bless us, O Lord, and these Thy gifts which of Thy bounty we are about to receive, through Christ Our Lord. Amen.

Grace After Meals

We give Thee thanks, O Almighty God, for all the benefits we have received from Thy bounty. Who lives and reigns world without end. Amen.

Act of Contrition

O my God, I am very sorry that I have sinned against Thee, for Thou art so good, and with Thy help I will not sin again.

Act of Faith

O my God, I firmly believe all the truths that the Holy Catholic Church believes and teaches. I believe these truths, O Lord, because Thou, the Infallible Truth, hast revealed them to her. In this Faith I am resolved to live and die. Amen.

Act of Hope

O my God, relying on Thy promises, I hope that, through the infinite merits of Jesus Christ, Thou wilt grant me pardon of my sins and the graces necessary to serve Thee in this life and to obtain eternal happiness in the next. Amen.

Appendices

Act of Charity

O my God, I love Thee with my whole heart and above all things, because Thou art infinitely good and perfect; and I love my neighbor as myself for love of Thee. Grant that I may love Thee more and more in this life and in the next for all eternity. Amen.

Hail, Holy Queen

Hail, Holy Queen, Mother of Mercy, hail our life, our sweetness and our hope! To thee do we cry, poor banished children of Eve; to thee do we send up our sighs, mourning and weeping in this valley of tears. Turn then, most gracious advocate, thine eyes of mercy toward us, and after this our exile, show unto us the blessed fruit of thy womb, Jesus. O clement, O loving, O sweet Virgin Mary. Amen.

The Memorare

Remember, O most gracious Virgin Mary, that never was it known in any age, that any one who fled to thy protection, implored thy help, or sought thy intercession, was left unaided. Inspired by this confidence, I fly to thee, O Virgin of virgins, my Mother, to thee do I come, before thee I stand sinful and sorrowful. O Mother of the Word Incarnate, despise not my petitions, but in thy mercy hear and answer them. Amen.

Prayer to St Michael

Saint Michael the Archangel, defend us in the hour of battle. Be our safeguard against the wickedness and snares of the devil. May God rebuke him, we humbly pray, and do thou, O Prince of the heavenly host, by the power of God cast into hell Satan and all the other wicked spirits that prowl about the world seeking the ruin of souls. Amen.

Guardian Angel Prayer

Angel of God, my guardian dear, to whom God's love commits me here: ever this day be at my side to light and guard, to rule and guide. Amen.

The Divine Praises

Blessed be God
Blessed be His Holy Name
Blessed be Jesus Christ true God and true Man
Blessed be the Name of Jesus
Blessed be His Most Sacred Heart
Blessed be His Most Precious Blood
Blessed be Jesus in the Most Holy Sacrament of the Altar
Blessed be the Holy Spirit, the Paraclete
Blessed be the great Mother of God, Mary Most Holy
Blessed be Her Holy and Immaculate Conception
Blessed be Her Glorious Assumption
Blessed be the Name of Mary, Virgin and Mother
Blessed be St. Joseph, Her Most Chaste Spouse
Blessed be God in His Angels and in His Saints. Amen.

Prayer to the Holy Spirit

V. Come, Holy Spirit, fill the hearts of Thy faithful.
R. And enkindle in them the fire of Thy love.
V. Send forth Thy Spirit and they shall be created.
R. And Thou shalt renew the face of the earth.

Let us pray

O God, Who has taught the hearts of the faithful by the light of the Holy Spirit, grant that in the same Spirit we may be truly wise and ever rejoice in His consolation. Through Christ Our Lord. Amen.

About the Author

Robert M. Haddad holds qualifications in law, theology, philosophy and religious education, namely, a LL.B (USyd.), Grad. Cert. in RE (Charles Sturt Uni.), Grad. Dip. Ed. (ACU), Grad. Dip. in Teacher Ed. (College of Teachers, London), AMLP (Oxon.), MA Theo. Studies (UNDA – University Medalist), MRelEd (UNDA) and a M. Phil (ACU). For his M. Phil. Robert researched the apologetical arguments of St Justin Martyr.

In addition to his studies, Robert has also authored various books, including *Lord of History Series* (2 volumes), *The Apostles' Creed*, *The Family and Human Life*, *Defend the Faith!*, *The Case for Christianity – St Justin Martyr's Arguments for Religious Liberty and Judicial Justice*, *Answering the Anti-Catholic Challenge* (ch. 3) and *1001 Reasons Why it's Great to be Catholic!*

From 1990-2005, Robert worked full-time at St Charbel's College, Sydney, teaching Religion and History. He held the positions of Year Co-ordinator and Religious Education Co-ordinator concurrently for ten years and was Assistant Principal (Welfare) for six years.

From 2006-2008, Robert worked full-time as the Convener of the Catholic Chaplaincy at the University of Sydney. He was also a lecturer at the Center for Thomistic Studies for eleven years (1996-2008), teaching Apologetics, Church Fathers and Church History, as well as assisting part-time with *Lumen Verum Apologetics* (1996-present) and the Catholic Adult Education Centre (2010-2013).

From 2009-2012, Robert was the Director of the Confraternity of Christian Doctrine (Sydney) and in that capacity was the chief editor of the revised *Christ our Light and Life* (3rd Edition) religious education K-12 curriculum used by Catholic students in state schools as well as the *Gratia Series* sacramental programs for children preparing for Reconciliation, First Holy Communion, and Confirmation in the Archdiocese of Sydney. He has recently also edited a new RCIA resource for use in Catholic schools in the same Archdiocese entitled *Initiate*.

In 2014, Robert was awarded an Australia Day Award by the Australia Day Council of New South Wales for his overall contribution to education. Currently, he is the Head of New Evangelization for the Catholic Education Office (Sydney) and lectures/tutors in Theology at the University of Notre Dame, Sydney. From time to time Robert also appears on the Telepace Television Network and Voice of Charity radio.

Other Works by the Author

Introduction to the Greatest Fathers of the Church (Parousia Media, 1999)

A Seat at the Supper (General Editor; author Frank Colyer, self-published, 2001)

Introduction to Early Church History (Parousia Media, 2002)

The Apostles' Creed (Parousia Media, 2004)

The Case for Christianity – St Justin Martyr's Arguments for Religious Liberty and Judicial Justice (Connor Court Publishing, 2009)

The Family and Human Life (2nd Ed. co-authored with Bernard Toutounji, Parousia Media, 2011)

Defend the Faith! (Parousia Media, 2012)

Answering the Anti-Catholic Challenge (General Editor and author of ch. 3, Modotti Press, 2012)

1001 Reasons Why it's Great to be Catholic! (Parousia Media, 2014)

Christ our Light and Life (General Editor 3rd Edition, 2012) religious education curriculum K-12 used by Catholic students in government schools throughout the state of New South Wales.

Gratia Series (General Editor, 2012) sacramental programs for children preparing for Reconciliation, First Holy Communion, and Confirmation in the Archdiocese of Sydney.

Initiate (General Editor, CEO Sydney Publications, 2014), a RCIA resource for use in Catholic schools in the Archdiocese of Sydney.

www.ingramcontent.com/pod-product-compliance
Lightning Source LLC
Chambersburg PA
CBHW071625080526
44588CB00010B/1272